IN THE
SHADOW
OF THE
CROSS

IN THE SHADOW OF THE CROSS

Walk with Jesus
from the Garden to the Tomb

RANDAL EARL DENNY

Beacon Hill Press of Kansas City
Kansas City, Missouri

10   9   8   7   6   5   4   3   2   1

To Dr. W. T. Purkiser,
college president and seminary professor,
who inspired—and insisted—
that I write my sermons
each week
and who modeled
the gentleness of Jesus

Contents

Preface

In 24 hours how could things deteriorate so quickly? From a banquet to a burial! The dark shadow of the executioner's cross sliced across that unforgettable day. A tragic day—yet planned by a sovereign God before this old world was steady on its feet. The shadow of that cross reached back to the early pages of Genesis. God forewarned the serpent of temptation: "And I will put enmity between you and the woman, and between your offspring and hers; He will crush your head, and you will strike his heel" (Gen. 3:15).

Here and there the parchments of the past revealed the shadow of the cross: "But he was pierced for our transgressions, he was crushed for our iniquities; the punishment that brought us peace was upon him, and by his wounds we are healed" (Isa. 53:5).

Leading up to Easter Sunday morning, the Christian's dawning of hope and sunburst of joy, my people and I walked together from the Garden of Gethsemane to the borrowed tomb. We watched as Jesus prayed His prayer of submission to the Father's will, as Jesus passed through the sting of betrayal, as Jesus faced undaunted the inhumane treatment of hatred, and as Jesus spoke unexpected last words—a legacy of love. The shadow of the Cross is the anguished prelude to the best news we ever heard: "He has risen!" (Mark 16:6).

Acknowledgments

A word of appreciation to my wife, Ruth, who encourages me to keep writing. Her boost of my preaching ministry is a valuable asset to me.

A word of thanks to my congregation at Spokane Valley Church—"What a Jesus we have in friends!"

IN THE SHADOW OF THE CROSS

1

VICTORY THROUGH SURRENDER

MATTHEW 26:36-46
CF. MARK 14:32-42; LUKE 22:39-46

Then Jesus went with his disciples to a place called Gethsemane, and he said to them, "Sit here while I go over there and pray." He took Peter and the two sons of Zebedee along with him, and he began to be sorrowful and troubled. Then he said to them, "My soul is overwhelmed with sorrow to the point of death. Stay here and keep watch with me."

Going a little farther, he fell with his face to the ground and prayed, "My Father, if it is possible, may this cup be taken from me. Yet not as I will, but as you will" *(Matt. 26:36-39)*.

An angel from heaven appeared to him and strengthened him. And being in anguish, he prayed more earnestly, and his sweat was like drops of blood falling to the ground *(Luke 22:43-44)*.

Then he returned to his disciples and found them sleeping. "Could you men not keep watch with me for one hour?" he asked Peter. "Watch and pray so that you will not fall into temptation. The spirit is willing, but the body is weak."

He went away a second time and prayed, "My Father, if it is not possible for this cup to be taken away unless I drink it, may your will be done."

> When he came back, he again found them sleep-
> ing, because their eyes were heavy. So he left them
> and went away once more and prayed the third time,
> saying the same thing.
>
> Then he returned to the disciples and said to
> them, "Are you still sleeping and resting? Look, the
> hour is near, and the Son of Man is betrayed into the
> hands of sinners. Rise, let us go! Here comes my be-
> trayer!" *(Matt. 26:40-46).*

In transoceanic flight there is a point pilots refer to as "the point of no return." When this particular spot is crossed, it is closer to continue on ahead than to turn back. At that moment there is nothing left to do but go forward.

For Jesus that moment came in the Garden of Gethsemane. That hour of decision would mark the destiny of His life. He had reached His point of no return!

Preaching on this Gethsemane experience, Dr. John Henry Jowett commented to his congregation: "And now I lead you by a path that I almost fear to tread."

When an old church building in Richmond, Virginia, was torn down, workmen found a stained-glass picture of Jesus praying in Gethsemane. An earlier generation had covered the window with organ pipes, and the brick wall of a neighboring structure obscured it on the outside. Nearly everyone had forgotten it was there.

But for students of the Bible, Jesus praying in Gethsemane remains holy ground. There is mystery about it. An awesome atmosphere makes us catch our breath lest we disturb the sanctity of that moment! We feel that more has gone on than meets the eye. Jesus uttered the most important prayer we can offer: "Not my will, but yours be done" (Luke 22:42). It is not the cry of defeat, but the declaration of total submission: victory through surrender!

Dr. E. Stanley Jones observed, "Everybody surrenders—surrenders to something, someone or [the Savior]."[1] Jesus at prayer in Gethsemane wrestled over the issue:

would He bypass the Cross, or would He willingly take up His cross? Would He shun the shame of bearing the world's sin or give himself sacrificially in love? At Gethsemane, the Master kneels at the crossroads of eternity!

One preacher said:

> When we think of the praying Christ, many of us hold in our minds a most familiar picture, a . . . picture of Jesus praying in the Garden of Gethsemane, seen in many churches. I would not wish to destroy any inspiration a person may have received from it, but the next time you see it, notice something. A halo is about Jesus' head. Light streams in from above. He looks up serene and calm. The picture looks very holy, but it is not very real.
>
> The halo makes Jesus different from us! So does the light. We have no halos. We are ordinary people. We have no light streaming at us from above, not in that way. Prayer for us is effort, exertion, struggle. Was it not that for Jesus? What actually happened in Gethsemane when He sweat, as it were, great drops of blood—was that not struggle? Effort? He had no halo! The moment Jesus receives a halo and light, He is no longer the human Jesus of the gospels. We destroy the whole gospel story. We deny that Jesus is man, actually man, so completely man that He *needs* to pray![2]

The Bible says, "During the days of Jesus' life on earth, he offered up prayers and petitions with loud cries and tears to the one who could save him from death, and he was heard because of his reverent submission" (Heb. 5:7).

Gethsemane is the place of openness, brokenness, and yieldedness!

THE PLACE OF OPENNESS

Leaving the comforting presence of His special friends, Jesus opened himself to God. On the eve of crisis, Jesus prayed alone, "My Father, if it is possible, may this cup be taken from me" (Matt. 26:39). Jesus was as human as you and me. The tragedy of suffering and dying loomed ahead. Jesus spoke honestly with God: "What are You saying, Father? I don't like it—but I am listening!"

Sometimes God's direction for us demands high cost. Persecution has taken many forms. It hurts to suffer over one's own mistakes and sins, but it is agony to suffer for the mistakes and sins of *others!* Through it all, we must keep open to God. We must not shut Him out or drown out His voice with our objections.

It is not sin against God to question Him, to lament misfortune, to doubt the rightness of a situation. To express our hesitancy, to verbalize our fears, and to struggle over our limited understanding underlines our dependence upon a great and powerful God.

Like Jesus, we must realistically face whatever God calls us to. There's no reason to pretend that genuine discipleship is lighthearted and easy. The high cost of discipleship is exceeded only by the high cost of low living!

My friend C. S. Cowles said, "Jesus faced the cup. He did not try to pretend that its bitter contents did not exist. Nor did He seek mystic flights of spiritual escape. The cup had come to Him, not by His choice or decision, but in the course of faithfully doing the Father's will. He shrank from its implications."[3]

As He struggled with God's will, Jesus got up three times and went back to look at His sleeping disciples, so weak and weary. It gave Him a perspective on God's purposes: He must accept God's will for their sakes. Even though sleeping, they believed on Him, trusted Him, and put their fortunes on Him. Jesus knew He must drink the cup of death in order for His men to drink the cup of life!

Jesus based His openness to God on a trusting relationship. He prayed, "My Father." Even in the face of suffering, Jesus knew that God was no distant, hostile God—but His intimate, caring Father. Our view of God makes a great difference in how we face tough places in life.

I love my two girls. Suppose that when I came home

when they were small they said to me, "Daddy, we missed you. We've decided to do anything you desire. You tell us and we'll do it."

If I had answered the way many people view God's reaction to our consecration, I would have grabbed them, shaken them hard, and shouted, "I've been waiting for this chance! I'll make you regret this decision as long as you live. I'm going to take all the fun out of your life. You'll eat turnips three times a day if you serve me!"

No—not at all. You know what I would do: because I'm their father, I would put my arms around them and love them. I would do my best to demonstrate my love. I would guide them into the best possible, most fruitful life. And I'm only a man with limitations and poor judgment. I can't even express my love as adequately and completely as God does.

Our God reaches down with His infinite compassion, helps us in our deepest needs, and demonstrates in a thousand ways that He loves us. We have nothing to fear by opening ourselves to Him: "Not my will, but thine, be done!" (Luke 22:42, KJV).

We must learn to be open to God's will. God is not controlled by His power. He exercises His power, but He is guided by His wisdom. If we remain open to God, we allow His wisdom to work in our lives. We are enriched by the wisdom of "our Father."

As we pray, "Not my will, but yours be done," we are saying, "Lord, I am available!"

THE PLACE OF BROKENNESS

Even the name, "Gethsemane," is a clue to what happens there. The Hebrew word "Gethsemane" means "olive mill" or "olive press." Not only was it the Mount of Olives where olives grew in silver-green orchards beneath sunlit skies, but also it was there ripe olives were broken and crushed. Out of the experience of brokenness flowed precious olive oil for food and health, for lamplight, and as an ointment for healing.

In this place of brokenness, Jesus passed through crushing agony. It pleased the Lord to bruise Him and crush Him so that the fresh oil of the Holy Spirit might soon flow to all who believe on Him. His oil of blessing nourishes our spirits, gives light to those in darkness, and brings healing to the heartaches of humanity.

Gethsemane, the place of brokenness, brings to mind the words of the Lord to Isaiah: "I have trodden the winepress alone; from the nations no one was with me. . . . I looked, but there was no one to help, I was appalled that no one gave support" (63:3, 5).

Jesus left eight men near the gateway to the Garden of Gethsemane. He took three men up the hill a little farther: Peter, James, and John. Why did He select them? Had not all three recently boasted of their willingness to suffer or serve for the Master? If Jesus had asked them to perform some great heroic duty, they would have done it. Yet they got drowsy when Jesus only asked them to "watch with me for one hour" (Matt. 26:40). I think Jesus yearned to have them near for comfort and support in His lonely hour of spiritual battle.

Earlier, Jesus had taken these same three fellows up the Mount of Transfiguration. They witnessed His glory on the mountaintop. And now Jesus knows they must prepare to share in His suffering. If you and I expect to reign with Him, we should not be surprised to suffer with Him.

> *Must Jesus bear the cross alone,*
> *And all the world go free?*
> *No, there's a cross for ev'ryone,*
> *And there's a cross for me.*
> —Thomas Shepherd and others

The apostle Paul exclaimed, "I want to know Christ and the power of his resurrection and the fellowship of sharing in his sufferings, becoming like him in his death" (Phil. 3:10). He will give us grace and glory!

Jesus demonstrated that there is a place of brokenness before God. Matthew described it: "And he began to be sorrowful and troubled" (26:37). A spirit of heaviness pressed on Him like a lead weight. He would be broken by the weight of bearing the sins of the world! Already it was crushing Him. Jesus bore my sins—every one of them. He was taking on yours too. The Master cried out to His intimate companions, "My soul is overwhelmed with sorrow to the point of death. Stay here and keep watch with me" (v. 38).

In that Eastern culture, the usual position for prayer was standing, but Jesus, broken before God, fell to His knees! It was not the religious curtsy performed so mechanically, but rather the violence of His personal struggle. Jesus agonized over our sins. How can we be so nonchalant about them?

God can't fully use us until our proud self is broken. The unyielding, unteachable self justifies itself. It demands its own way, stands up for its rights, and seeks its own glory. That self within must be broken before the Lord. We must die to self-will. Brokenness is our humble response to God's conviction in our hearts. Jesus, having enjoyed heaven's splendor, gave it all up to come down among us, being obedient even unto death—death on a cross. He was willing to be broken for us. Paul admonishes, "Your attitude should be the same as that of Christ Jesus" (Phil. 2:5).

A man said to his Christian friend, "I've absolutely hit bottom. All my strength is gone!" For nearly 30 minutes he told of all the things that had knocked him down. Then he added, "I've hit bottom. I can't go any further down. I have to admit I can't handle my life any longer."

His Christian friend asked, "Is that it? Have you really hit bottom?"

"Yes," the discouraged man replied. "Isn't that awful?"

"Awful?" his companion responded. "Not on your life! That's wonderful. I congratulate you!"

"What do you mean? I just told you I've hit bottom. Why do you congratulate me?"

The Christian explained, "Because there's no place quite like the bottom. You can't go down any further. That's it. That's the stopping place. Good, firm, substantial bottom—and you're right smack on it! Congratulations, because the only direction you can go from now on is up! Your future is directly ahead of you—up! So, thank God you've hit bottom and you're not going any further down!"

The startled man asked, "But what about not having any more strength? I can't handle my life anymore."

The friend added, "That's simply wonderful too. It means you're at the place where you're ready to put your life in the hands of One who can take charge of it—Jesus Christ."

In his desperation and brokenness before God, that man was introduced to a Heavenly Father who began to help him put life back together.

If you will be open and honest with God, He will show you your real self. When we admit that God is right about us, we find ourselves at a place of brokenness! Then, and only then, comes His healing touch.

When we pray "Not my will, but yours be done," we are saying, "Lord, I am dependent."

THE PLACE OF YIELDEDNESS

Jesus prayed, "Nevertheless, not my will, but thine, be done" (Luke 22:42, KJV). His was a prayer of surrender, of relinquishment to God.

Jesus' prayer of yieldedness contains a special note hidden in translation. The grammatical construction of the verb "be done" means literally, "Thy will keep on being done." In other words, this prayer of surrender wasn't just for that moment—the present crisis—but it is a yield-edness as a way of life. When I pray it as Jesus said it, I mean "I surrender or yield it all now and will keep it surrendered and yielded day in and day out." A person doesn't say, "Not my will, but yours be done" only in the great Gethsemanes of life but must learn to pray it through all of life's trials and decisions.

The attitude in which you say "Your will be done" makes a difference. You might say in an attitude of help-less submission, caught in the jaws of fate, "Thy will be done." Or you might say it as one whipped into line as an admission of total defeat! Or you might say "Thy will be done" in utter frustration that your dream will never come true, that all hope is gone, that you are left with only bleak regret. Perhaps with bitterness in surrender, you feel he can't do anything else.

However, you can say "Thy will be done" with the joy-ful assent of perfect trust and obedience. That's how Jesus said it—as one talking to His Father, whose everlasting arms underneath held Him steady. Jesus yielded to a love that would never let Him go! God will mend your broken heart if you will give Him all the pieces!

Jesus' prayer did not express a passive submission to His Father. He prayed with determination to allow God's will to take precedence. Jesus yielded in order to follow God's purposes for His life—and ours.

When Julius Caesar sailed across the English Channel with his Roman legions, they were turned back at first by the Saxons. They made a second attempt to conquer the British Isles, but the Saxons, looking down from the cliffs, drove them away. The third time, however, once the Ro-man soldiers arrived on shore with all their equipment, Caesar ordered every one of their ships burned behind them. The men watched their own ships burn to the wa-terline and sink.

With the last hope of retreat gone, the soldiers

marched straight ahead into the fury of the Saxons, though greatly outnumbered. The Saxons ran away. Total commitment—yieldedness without retreat—left them with great determination to win. The Romans had no choice but to advance—and conquer!

Our Gethsemane experiences demand that kind of yieldedness and submission to God's purposes. I like the spirit of the gospel song that says:

> *Thou didst hear my plea so kindly;*
> *Thou didst grant me so much grace.*
> *Ev'ry bridge is burned behind me;*
> *I will ne'er my steps retrace.*
> —Johnson Oatman, Jr.

The place of surrender is never easy. We must face the fact of the cross in our lives. It demands sacrifice. However, the victory of Jesus' cross was won in prayer during His Gethsemane experience. His actions on the morrow, facing trial, disgrace, and crucifixion, merely carried out His decision made in Gethsemane: "My Father, if it is not possible for this cup to be taken away unless I drink it, may your will be done" (Matt. 26:42; cf. Luke 22:42).

Did God answer His prayer? True, God did not remove the cup of suffering and death. But God did hear Him and answered His prayer: "An angel from heaven appeared to him and strengthened him" (Luke 22:43). God enabled Jesus not to be overwhelmed with discouragement nor to fail. From this point on until His death, you can sense that Jesus was strengthened and calmed. He is obviously in control. Jesus had the regal bearing of a king—even in death!

A musician commented on Chopin's "Nocturne in C# Minor": "In this piece all is sorrow and trouble. Oh, such sorrow and trouble! Until [Chopin] begins to speak to God, to pray; then it is all right!"

So it was with Jesus. He walked into Gethsemane in the dark. He came out in the light—because He talked with God. "He went into Gethsemane in . . . agony; He came out with the victory won, and with peace in His soul—because He had talked with God."[4]

We can know that our surrender is complete. We shall experience inner peace and rest and the sweet presence of the Holy Spirit strengthening within. Our struggle with surrender is tempered by Jesus' victory. His victory was our gain! Charles Allen noted, "The prayer of our Lord, 'Nevertheless not my will, but thine, be done' (Luke 22:42) is not insurance against some Calvary, but it is a guarantee of an Easter. That prayer is no protection against struggle and pain, but it is assurance of final triumph."[5]

My friend Maurice Hall, former missionary to Africa, wrote in his Bible many years ago: "Dear God: Anything, anywhere, anytime, somehow!" And Maurice signed his name. This was his vivid reminder of total submission to God for life and eternity.

E. Stanley Jones concluded, "Whether it is a once-for-all surrender in a life crisis or a day-by-day surrender of the problems of life as they come up, the way out is—victory through surrender."[6]

As we pray, "Not my will, but yours be done," we are saying, "Lord, I am Yours!"

Will you make this your sincere prayer?

Not my will, but Thine; not my will, but Thine;
Not my will, but Thy will be done, Lord, in me.
May Thy Spirit divine fill this being of mine.
Not my will, but Thy will be done, Lord, in me. *

—Hugh C. Benner

2

MUTINY!

MATTHEW 26:47-56
CF. MARK 14:43-52; LUKE 22:47-53; JOHN 18:1-12

When he had finished praying, Jesus left with his disciples and crossed the Kidron Valley. On the other side there was an olive grove, and he and his disciples went into it.

Now Judas, who betrayed him, knew the place, because Jesus had often met there with his disciples. So Judas came to the grove, guiding a detachment of soldiers and some officials from the chief priests and Pharisees. They were carrying torches, lanterns and weapons.

Jesus, knowing all that was going to happen to him, went out and asked them, "Who is it you want?"

"Jesus of Nazareth," they replied.

"I am he," Jesus said. (And Judas the traitor was standing there with them.) When Jesus said, "I am he," they drew back and fell to the ground.

Again he asked them, "Who is it you want?"

And they said, "Jesus of Nazareth."

"I told you that I am he," Jesus answered. "If you are looking for me, then let these men go." This happened so that the words he had spoken would be fulfilled: "I have not lost one of those you gave me" *(John 18:1-9)*.

Now the betrayer had arranged a signal with them: "The one I kiss is the man; arrest him." Going at once to Jesus, Judas said, "Greetings, Rabbi!" and kissed him *(Matt. 26:48-49)*.

But Jesus asked him, "Judas, are you betraying the Son of Man with a kiss?" *(Luke 22:48).* "Friend, do what you came for."

Then the men stepped forward, seized Jesus and arrested him *(Matt. 26:50).*

When Jesus' followers saw what was going to happen, they said, "Lord, should we strike with our swords?" *(Luke 22:49).*

Then Simon Peter, who had a sword, drew it and struck the high priest's servant, cutting off his right ear. (The servant's name was Malchus) *(John 18:10).*

But Jesus answered, "No more of this!" And he touched the man's ear and healed him *(Luke 22:51).*

"Put your sword back in its place," Jesus said to him, "for all who draw the sword will die by the sword. Do you think I cannot call on my Father, and he will at once put at my disposal more than twelve legions of angels? But how then would the Scriptures be fulfilled that say it must happen in this way?" *(Matt. 26:52-54).*

Then Jesus said to the chief priests, the officers of the temple guard, and the elders who had come for him, "Am I leading a rebellion, that you have come with swords and clubs? Every day I was with you in the temple courts, and you did not lay a hand on me. But this is your hour—when darkness reigns" *(Luke 22:52-53).* "But the Scriptures must be fulfilled" *(Mark 14:49).*

Then all the disciples deserted him and fled *(Matt. 26:56).*

A young man, wearing nothing but a linen garment, was following Jesus. When they seized him, he fled naked, leaving his garment behind *(Mark 14:51-52).*

"Mutiny!"—the dreaded word that describes lawlessness running rampant among seamen or soldiers. Mutiny is abandonment of authority. Mutiny is rejection of leadership. Jesus experienced mutiny by the kiss of a traitor.

However, this sudden treachery came as no surprise, for the psalmist had prophesied hundreds of years earlier: "Even my close friend, whom I trusted, he who shared my bread, has lifted up his heel against me" (Ps. 41:9).

The electrifying moment of mutiny occurred when Jesus faced Judas and his armed allies. This mutiny, like all sin, was a clenched fist in the face of God. Sin is man's declaration of independence from God.

Facing the mob, Jesus asked, "Why are you here?" (Matt. 26:50, RSV). Shakespeare mimicked this moment in his play *Julius Caesar* when Caesar turns to his good friend and asks, *"Et tu, Brute?"* ("And you, Brutus?"). In that instant of betrayal, Brutus plunges his dagger to assassinate his trusting friend and leader. Judas' betrayal of Jesus carries the same pathos and tragedy.

When order is destroyed, decency is lost. Mutiny breeds lawlessness; lawlessness spawns failure. Through all the facets of this mutiny, the repetition of human failure stands out.

THE FAILURE OF FORCE TO OVERCOME LOVE

The vanity of violence is the mistaken belief that violence can conquer real love. What a picture of contrasts!—Jesus serene and unshaken. The motley crowd masking their fears by mob rule: "We have come to take You by force, Jesus. We are taking everything away from You!'

"But I have come to lay down my life as a ransom for many. I already gave up everything for you!"

What an empty victory they experienced!

The spiritual power of divine love can never be destroyed by clubs and swords. He who was Truth announced, "I am the light of the world" (John 8:12).

Have you ever attempted to smash a ray of light with a stick? Violence trying to subdue truth is like battering away at God's sunshine. Sunshine always wins!

The captors arrived to arrest Jesus. This moment

gives a glimpse of Jesus' sense of humor. Temple guards and religious rulers tried sneaking into the Garden of Gethsemane with blazing torches in order to arrest Jesus in the night. Can't you visualize them creeping around like elephants hiding behind lilies? How can a mob sneak into a little garden anyway?

Jesus stepped out like a spectator and asked, "Whom are you looking for?"

They whispered back, "Jesus of Nazareth."

The Master grinned in the shadows. "I am He!" And they were so shocked they jumped back and fell down! And you think force can conquer love?

There's nothing to suggest that a miraculous power terrorized them. They felt so guilty that they trembled before the unhidden innocence of Jesus.

Jesus is no victim. He is the eternal Victor. Jesus volunteered to give himself long ago.

A man working in the coal mines was stricken in his lungs when he attempted to rescue trapped friends; the fume-filled mine subsequently damaged his health. A union agitator came around later and said, "So they took your health too?"

"No," said the old miner. "I gave it!"

Jesus gave His life. No man took it. He gave it for others—for you and me! Jesus had taught His men earlier, "A hired man will run when he sees a wolf coming and will leave the sheep . . . I am the Good Shepherd . . . I lay down my life for the sheep" (John 10:12, 14-15, TLB). It was not the force of His captors but rather His own submissiveness to God and love for us that brought Him to that moment of arrest.

After Jesus prayed "Not my will, but yours be done" (Luke 22:42), we notice a serenity about Him. It is amazing how Jesus walks among hate-filled men, forsaken by disappearing disciples, and He absorbs physical abuse—

yet He is unbowed and unafraid. Having settled the issues in Gethsemane with God, He alone can say:

> *In the fell clutch of circumstance,*
> *I have not winced nor cried aloud.*
> *Under the bludgeonings of chance*
> *My head is bloody, but unbow'd.*

> *It matters not how strait the gate,*
> *How charged with punishments the scroll,*
> *I am the master of my fate:*
> *I am the captain of my soul.*[1]

—William Ernest Henley

THE FAILURE OF RELIGION WITHOUT HEART

Judas approached Jesus and said, "Greetings, Rabbi!" (Matt. 26:49). He gave the usual complimentary greeting among the Jews, but Judas was pretending to wish Jesus continued health while planning His destruction. Judas had honey on his tongue but poison in his heart.

In the custom of the Eastern world, Judas kissed Jesus—in fact, the Greek grammar suggests that Judas kissed Jesus again and again. In attempting to conceal his mutiny, he overdid it! Judas obviously tried to give outward assurance of his discipleship. Jesus' pretended friends are always His worst enemies.

John Henry Jowett wrote,

> To use a kiss in the ministry of betrayal is like using a sacramental cup to poison a friend . . . Evil which wears its own clothes is sufficiently repulsive, but it is not nearly so repulsive as when it counterfeits goodness, and decks itself in adornments stolen from the wardrobe of virtue. If betrayal comes with a curse and a frown, we know how to interpret its approach, but when it comes with smiles and kisses it can deceive the very elect. The kiss of Judas wounded the Lord far more deeply than did the nails which fastened Him to the cross.[2]

Love is betrayed not by a kiss but by an evil heart. Jesus is betrayed even now by the person with a divided heart. He warned once, "Not everyone who says to me, 'Lord, Lord,' will enter the kingdom of heaven, but only he who does the will of my Father who is in heaven" (Matt. 7:21). The Master is betrayed in our day many times for less than 30 pieces of silver. Sometimes He is betrayed for a moment of ungodly pleasure, sometimes for the smile of a Christless world, sometimes for misplaced stewardship. Like Judas, a person may show an outward embrace of all that is good and holy, but lack of inner commitment betrays the mask.

Herbert Hoover said, "Words without actions are the assassins of idealism." God's dream for our community is betrayed by well-meaning people who possess only outward institutional religion.

We fool ourselves if we think we can hide behind masks and remain a double-minded person. The Bible says, "He is a double-minded man, unstable in all he does" (James 1:8). Judas appeared to be a friend of Jesus—but it was only a mask. As E. Stanley Jones put it, "Either the mask becomes us, or we become the mask."[3]

Religion without heart needs to be exposed—and the Holy Spirit will expose it. Søren Kierkegaard wrote, "There comes a midnight of the soul when he must unmask." For us, as well as Judas, that can be a shattering experience—but a necessary one.

How fascinating to think what Judas might have been! He stood so close to Jesus—but walked so very far from Him. Judas reminds us that one may stand at the threshold of life but still remain outside. Religion without heart fails the test of life. If you are "almost persuaded," you are "almost, but lost!" Though you may be rich in the trappings of external religion like Nicodemus, you, too, must be born again.

A personal friend and classmate of mine pointed out, "This betrayal is, actually, not a betrayal of Christ. Judas actually betrays himself. For any betrayal of God is, in final analysis, a betrayal of self. Sin carries a man to the brink of despair, and often beyond. But it offers no avenue of return to human decency. It is a one-way street. Instead of Judas closing the door on Christ, he closed it on himself."[4]

THE FAILURE OF DEFENDING JESUS INSTEAD OF REVEALING HIM

Seeing Jesus bound by the mob, Peter made good his boast to defend Jesus. He swished his sword around, aiming for the head of the fellow nearest to Jesus—but he missed his target and got only an ear! Peter demonstrated his zeal for defending Christ, but he lacked the good judgment to reveal Jesus. Peter was acting in the flesh, not in the Spirit.

Jesus didn't need to be defended. He could have called 12 legions of angels to set Him free. The Lord needed Peter to carry on the good news of Jesus. Christ desires to be revealed, not defended!

Peter's blunder was the inevitable result of failing to "watch and pray so that you will not fall into temptation" (Matt. 26:41). Like Peter, we often try to settle issues by some forceful way instead of by staying awake to pray first. Jesus tells us, "I will build my church" (16:18). With the swish of our puny swords, we attempt to convince stubborn resisters of truth. Jesus said, "But I, when I am lifted up from the earth, will draw all men to myself" (John 12:32). He would rather have us reveal Him than defend Him. The only sword worth having is "the sword of the Spirit, which is the word of God" (Eph. 6:17).

Dr. William McCumber commented: "The command 'put up . . . thy sword,' followed by the statement that all who use the sword will die by it, forbids to the disciples of

Jesus the use of violence and arms to achieve Kingdom objectives. Unfortunately, the Church has often disobeyed, and its march through history has left a trailmark of one-eared men."[5]

I wonder: How often do we fail to reveal Jesus because we fear that we don't know how to defend Him? Many people have forfeited the joy of leading friends to Jesus out of fear of inadequacy in defending Jesus. To witness should not be an occasional consideration but rather a way of life.

The Master longs for us to reveal Him in our poor world. Marcia Skinner, missionary wife in the Republic of South Africa, wrote:

Bedtime. I kneel between two small boys and listen as two boy-sized prayers are offered to a God whose ear is listening for boy-sized requests.

"Mommy," my six-year-old boy says earnestly, "you're Jesus for us. We can't see Jesus, and you're the one who tells us the right things to do."

Startled, I recognize the thought beneath his groping words and explain to him that Mommy knows Jesus and has studied His teachings in the Bible; and this is the way Jesus helps her to guide him.

But his words print themselves indelibly on my mind. Lord, how accurate a mirror am I of Your love, Your care, to my children? How carefully do I reflect Your patience in accepting interruptions, even from a child? How many times have I distorted Your image to watchful, trusting eyes? Is the concept of You my children are storing in their memories a true one? To be Jesus to them until they are mature enough to grasp the difference between You and a disciple who longs to be Christlike but often falls short—what a heavy, yet blessed responsibility!

There are others. In their hunger for reality, their minds cry out, "We would see Jesus. In your living, Missionary, in your attitudes, in your reactions, be Jesus to us."[6]

Oh, to reflect His grace,
Causing the world to see
Love that will glow
Till others shall know
Jesus, revealed in me.*
—Gipsy Smith

Only Luke the physician notes that Jesus, at His moment of betrayal and arrest, performed His last miracle before being crucified. He healed the ear of Malchus, the wounded enemy of Jesus. This last act of divine compassion is performed by Jesus' tender touch. He healed a wound inflicted by the blundering zeal of an excited disciple.

The master didn't say to himself, "He's only a servant. And it's only an ear." Jesus doesn't know what small wounds are; He doesn't know what insignificant people are. If we learn to reveal Christ, we won't be opening so many wounds and hurting people by zealous blundering or stinging indifference.

The purpose of examining Judas' betrayal is not to pour more guilt on the failures of overly sensitive people. Its purpose is to point us all to One who stands ready to forgive failure, to offer understanding love, to heal broken hearts and broken relationships.

Sometime back, newspapers carried the story of a young fellow named William, who was a fugitive from the police. The teenager had run away with his girlfriend because the parents were trying to break them up.

What William didn't know was that an ailment that he had been seeing the doctor about was diagnosed, just after his disappearance, as cancer. Now, here was William, doing his best to elude the police, lest he lose his love, while they are doing their best to find him lest he lose his life. He thought they were after him to punish him; they were really after him to save his life.

William is representative of every man, whose guilt tells him God is after him to straight-jacket him in this life and torture him forever.[7]

Even in Judas' betrayal, God would have us see Jesus offering forgiveness and cleansing in order to make our new life worth living!

An Easter pageant, *The Christus,* is presented each year at Florida State Prison . . . Originally, at the finale, Judas fell to his knees before the Crucified, crying, "My Lord and my God, have mercy!" The applause [of the prisoners] greeting this climax was so vigorous and spontaneous that for a while the scene was omitted to preserve the dignity felt to be fitting. Now the programs carry the line: *Do not applaud* . . . Convicts do not want to believe that even Judas was hopeless. They do not want to believe that the Judas in them is beyond salvation . . . Christ on the Cross tells them that their deepest hope is valid . . . that they are not hopeless.[8]

Mutiny is not final. Failure is not forever. Even Judas could have found hope in Jesus—and we can too.

3

FAILURE, NOT A QUITTER

MATTHEW 26:58, 69-75
CF. MARK 14:54, 66-72; LUKE 22:54-62;
JOHN 18:15-18, 25-27

Peter followed him at a distance *(Mark 14:54)*. Simon Peter and another disciple were following Jesus. Because this disciple was known to the high priest, he went with Jesus into the high priest's courtyard, but Peter had to wait outside at the door. The other disciple, who was known to the high priest, came back, spoke to the girl on duty there and brought Peter in.

"You are not one of his disciples, are you?" the girl at the door asked Peter.

He replied, "I am not."

It was cold, and the servants and officials stood around a fire they had made to keep warm. Peter also was standing with them, warming himself *(John 18:15-18)*. He . . . sat down with the guards to see the outcome *(Matt. 26:58)*.

While Peter was below in the courtyard, one of the servant girls of the high priest came by. When she saw Peter warming himself, she looked closely at him.

"You also were with that Nazarene, Jesus," she said.

But he denied it. "I don't know or understand what you're talking about," he said, and went out into the entryway [and the rooster crowed—marginal note] *(Mark 14:66-68)*.

Then he went out to the gateway, where another girl saw him and said to the people there, "This fellow was with Jesus of Nazareth."

He denied it again, with an oath: "I don't know the man!" *(Matt. 26:71-72).*

One of the high priest's servants, a relative of the man whose ear Peter had cut off, challenged him, "Didn't I see you with him in the olive grove?"

Again Peter denied it *(John 18:26-27).*

A little later someone else saw him and said *(Luke 22:58),* "Surely you are one of them, for you are a Galilean" *(Mark 14:70),* "for your accent gives you away."

Then he began to call down curses on himself and he swore to them, "I don't know the man!" *(Matt. 26:73-74).*

Immediately the rooster crowed the second time *(Mark 14:72).*

The Lord turned and looked straight at Peter *(Luke 22:61).* Then Peter remembered the word Jesus had spoken *(Matt. 26:75):* "Before the rooster crows twice you will disown me three times." And he broke down and wept *(Mark 14:72).* And he went outside and wept bitterly *(Luke 22:62).*

It's better to try something and fail than to do nothing and succeed! It's difficult for a team to give its best on the field and then face defeat. You can avoid failure by not playing the game—but, of course, you forfeit the opportunity to win. If you're going to play the game, you must accept the possibility of winning and the possibility of losing.

Unlike his friends, Peter went where the action was. Except for young John and Peter, "all the disciples deserted him and fled" (Matt. 26:56). At great personal risk, Peter warmed his hands around the fire of Jesus' enemies—right in their courtyard. He did it because he cared what happened to Jesus.

As one commented, "Liability to temptation is the price that a man pays when he is adventurous in mind and action. It may well be that it is better to fail in a gallant enterprise than to run away and not even to attempt it."[1]

Peter possessed many good qualities. He willingly gave up all to follow Jesus. He obeyed without hesitation. One time Jesus said, "Put out into deep water, and let down the nets for a catch" (Luke 5:4).

Having fished all night, Peter knew no fish were around. But he replied, "Master, we've worked hard all night and haven't caught anything. But because you say so, I will let down the nets" (Luke 5:5).

Peter was a man of great faith. When Jesus came walking on the water, Peter alone stepped out, on the authority of Jesus' invitation. He was the first to gain the spiritual insight "You are the Christ, the Son of the living God" (Matt. 16:16).

Even though Peter stumbled and denied Jesus in a tight spot, one should remember: "It was love which riveted him there in spite of the fact that he had been recognized three times; it was love which made him remember the words of Jesus; it was love which sent him out into the night to weep his heart out . . . The basic and lasting impression of this whole story is not that of Peter's cowardice, but that of Peter's love."[2]

We are stronger than our weakest link! Our love for Jesus is more important to Him than our failures in the hour of weakness.

A young lady commented to me, "Peter is my favorite character in the Bible. He is so human. He is so much like me!"

Let's watch Peter in his hour of weakness.

IN HIS HOUR OF WEAKNESS, PETER WOULD NOT BE IDENTIFIED WITH JESUS

Peter followed Jesus from afar off. Though he was a disciple of Jesus, he didn't want anyone to know it. Peter was interested in Jesus, but not yet willing to be identified with Him. He loved Jesus, but he feared being singled out as one of His disciples.

A missionary asked a man of India what led to his decision to be baptized. He replied, "Like Peter, I've been walking too far from the Lord. I must walk close to Him. I want to get involved, and so I want to take baptism." In India, when a person is baptized, everyone knows he is identified with Jesus.

Peter found himself surrounded with people who lacked love and respect for Jesus. His unwillingness to be identified as a follower of Jesus got him caught in a moment of crisis. Nor can we live undetected for long in two worlds—the ungodly society and the kingdom of God. The speech of one world betrays you in the other. Peter underestimated the power of ridicule, the power of peer pressure, and his own reluctance to be singled out as different. I don't think Peter feared dangerous circumstances as much as he feared the opinions of people. He felt powerless before accusing men.

A mother and her kindergarten-aged daughter went grocery shopping. Outside the store as the mother carried a huge brown shopping bag, the little girl skipped along beside her. Suddenly the mother slipped on a patch of ice. Her arms flew out, and her legs shot up in the air as she fell. Scattered groceries rattled all over the ground. As she and a good Samaritan gathered everything, her eye began to swell shut from the blow against the sidewalk.

This forlorn lady went to the market's fish counter to get some ice to put on her eye. Only then did she notice her little girl—embarrassed over having a mother who drew so much ridiculous attention. The child had scampered clear across the store and was examining fruit so no one would think she belonged to such a clumsy mother.

How quickly Peter disassociated himself from the spectacle of Jesus being bound, led away, and tormented! The shocking sight of Jesus being spit upon and slapped around made Peter ashamed to identify with Him.

What would you do in a crowd where people laughed

at Jesus, ridiculed His followers, scorned His teachings, and were critical of the Bible as God's Word? What would you say if someone in an irreverent crowd asked you, "Aren't you one of those Christians?" How would you react? What would you do then with Jesus?

A young man came to his pastor and said, "I was with a group that began to roar with laughter at the Christian faith. I just got up and left—and came here to talk with you."

The pastor asked, "You did right to leave, but, tell me, what would you have done if they had asked, 'Aren't you one of Christ's followers?' What would you have done?"

The young man replied thoughtfully, "I hope I would have said: 'I am. And it hurts me to hear what you are saying and doing.' I hope I would have said that."

IN HIS HOUR OF WEAKNESS, PETER FAILED IN HIS OWN STRENGTH

It seems that all night long Peter was trying to advance the cause of Christ in his own wisdom and in his own physical strength. From boasting of his loyalty to swinging his poorly aimed sword, Peter was trying to do God's work in Peter's way. When Jesus needed him to pray, he slept. When Jesus needed a witness, he warmed himself at the fireside of Jesus' enemies and denied friendship with Jesus.

Peter first pretended that he didn't understand what the girl was asking. Then he denied following Jesus. That led to him making an oath to swear by God as his witness that he didn't even know Jesus. He supported that terrible untruth of denial with curses: "If what I say isn't true, may God's curses be on me!" One denial seemed to call for another.

One person standing by the fire said to Peter, "Your speech betrays you. Your accent gives you away!" His Galilean accent was a dead giveaway. Thomas Hardy characterized it:

*"O come, come!" laughed the constables. "Why, man,
you speak the dialect*
> *He uses in His answers; you can hear Him up the stairs.*
> *So own it. We sha'n't hurt ye. There He's speaking now!
His syllables*
> *Are those you sound yourself when you are talking un-
awares,*
> *As this pretty girl declares."*

*"And you shudder when His chain clinks!" she rejoined.
"Oh yes, I noticed it.*
> *And you winced, too, when those cuffs they gave Him
echoed to us here."*[3]

Does your speech give you away as a follower of Jesus?

Whatever Peter's reasons for sneaking inside the high priest's courtyard, it led to failure. Peter's unsurrendered self had gotten the best of him again. He who had left his boats and nets to follow Jesus had not yet left his old self-ruling nature. Overconfident, Peter had assured himself, "Denying Jesus is one thing I will never do!"

History is full of cities and fortresses thought to be unconquerable, but attacked and scaled at the very spot of apparent strength. Overconfident, the defenders were carelessly off their guard. Satan attacks at the very point where you are quite confident of yourself—that's exactly where you are least likely to be careful.

One man confessed, "I fell because I deemed myself above temptation."

There lurks in everyone sometime or another the sad cry, "How could I ever have done it?"

Operating in his own strength, Peter failed miserably—but his was a failure of actions, not a failure of love. Peter has been often portrayed as a man who fell from grace, lost by his own failure. Instead, Peter was a disciple of Jesus. He loved Christ more than his moment of crisis portrayed. He failed in his performance, but he was not abandoned by the Lord. And God does not abandon *us* in *our* moment of failure.

A little girl wished to give her mother a special Mother's Day gift, but she had no money. However, she had a little china doll. Since she valued that doll so much, she was quite certain it was worth a lot of money. On her way to sell her doll at the store, she slipped and fell. Her china doll broke into pieces. On Mother's Day, all she had to give was broken fragments of her little doll, wrapped in the pain of disappointment. However, in Mother's eyes that was the most precious gift of all. In love, she overlooked her child's failure of perfect performance. How much more does God in love overlook our imperfect actions!

IN HIS HOUR OF WEAKNESS, PETER REMAINED TENDER TOWARD JESUS

H. G. Wells said, "A man may be a bad musician, and yet be passionately in love with music."[4] Regardless of Peter's failure, he was passionately devoted to Jesus Christ. William Barclay said, "There is hope for the man who even when he is sinning is still haunted by goodness."[5]

We must not be quick to judge Peter! Soon he will be filled with the Spirit of God at the festival of Pentecost. Thousands will be converted to Jesus Christ. It is wrong to give up on a fellow because he fails in one critical hour. George W. Truett commented, "We must not wash our hands of him. The Lord does not reject us when we fail Him, even though we fail Him again and again."[6] As always, the Master reaches out to offer mercy and grace through His love to all who repent of their failure.

Jesus does not reject us over an act of failure. He never abandons hope that we'll make it by trusting Him instead of ourselves. As Jesus was being led away, He turned and looked at Peter. It was not the look of disdain, nor the scowling glance of scorn. It was the look of love. Clarence Macartney said, "It was the look of wounded love, the love that still loved him despite his cruel and cowardly lie, the love that would not let him go." We must not forget: "The penalty of sin is to face, not the anger of sin, but the heart-break in His eyes."[7] I agree with Barclay:

It was the real Peter who protested his loyalty in the Upper Room; it was the real Peter who drew his lonely sword in the moonlight of the garden; it was the real Peter who followed Jesus, because he could not leave his Lord alone; it was *not* the real Peter who cracked beneath the tension and who denied his Lord. *And that is just what Jesus could see.* The tremendous thing about Jesus is that beneath all our failures He sees the real man. Jesus understands.[8]

No one understands like Jesus;
  He's a Friend beyond compare.
Meet Him at the throne of mercy;
  He is waiting for you there....

No one understands like Jesus,
  When you falter on the way.
Though you fail Him, sadly fail Him,
  He will pardon you today.*
—John W. Peterson

An old Anglican preacher reminds us: "Don't ever forget that the look of Jesus, however wonderful, would have been no good if, at the moment, Simon had not been looking His way."[9] Peter's heart remained tender toward his Master. Peter continued watching, looking, caring.

Something in Jesus' wonderful look of love suddenly struck Peter's heart. "And he went outside and wept bitterly" (Matt. 26:75). That's the response of the imperfect Christian—sensitive and tender toward Jesus, willing to admit failure. If Peter had not been a disciple of Jesus, he wouldn't have cared that much. "It takes a man with real

---

*"No One Understands like Jesus." Copyright 1952, renewed 1980 by John W. Peterson Music Company. All rights reserved. Used by permission.

courage to face up to his wrong. It takes a man of genuine heart to allow the tears of sorrow to wash his soul."[10] Heartbroken, Peter repented of his failure. Through his tears he saw the rainbow of hope.

The Bible says, "Godly sorrow brings repentance that leads to salvation and leaves no regret, but worldly sorrow brings death" (2 Cor. 7:10). Peter was deeply moved by his failure—and he repented of it. He no longer would be dogged with regret.

God's bookkeeping system on His children is very poor—He not only forgives but forgets! There's no need to continue dredging up our failures and sins of the past. John wrote, "My dear children, I write this to you so that you will not sin. But if anybody does sin, we have one who speaks to the Father in our defense—Jesus Christ, the Righteous One" (1 John 2:1).

When we fail, Jesus our Advocate speaks on our behalf in spite of our failure. Satan may accuse and whisper doubts about our relationship with God. But Jesus wants to know, "Do you love Me?"

No one is exempt from failure.

Behind our effort to try to impress God is the feeling that God will not love us the way we are. And we fall prey to that feeling because we live in a world of people who make us try to earn their love by conforming to their expectations for us. Since we tend to go through life auditioning for the love of others, it seems only natural that we would have to do the same thing with God. But the greatest discovery in life is that nothing in our minds or hearts or actions is hidden from God, and He still loves us.[11]

4

THE INEVITABLE QUESTION ABOUT THE INESCAPABLE CHRIST

MATTHEW 27:2, 11-26
CF. MARK 15:1-5; LUKE 23:1-5, 13-25; JOHN 18:28—19:16

Then the Jews led Jesus from Caiaphas to the palace of the Roman governor. By now it was early morning, and to avoid ceremonial uncleanness the Jews did not enter the palace; they wanted to be able to eat the Passover. So Pilate came out to them and asked, "What charges are you bringing against this man?"

"If he were not a criminal," they replied, "we would not have handed him over to you."

Pilate said, "Take him yourselves and judge him by your own law."

"But we have no right to execute anyone," the Jews objected. This happened so that the words Jesus had spoken indicating the kind of death he was going to die would be fulfilled *(John 18:28-32)*.

And they began to accuse him, saying, "We have found this man subverting our nation. He opposes payment of taxes to Caesar and claims to be Christ, a king" *(Luke 23:2)*.

Pilate then went back inside the palace, summoned Jesus and asked him, "Are you the king of the Jews?"

"Is that your own idea," Jesus asked, "or did others talk to you about me?"

"Am I a Jew?" Pilate replied. "It was your people and your chief priests who handed you over to me. What is it you have done?"

Jesus said, "My kingdom is not of this world. If it were, my servants would fight to prevent my arrest by the Jews. But now my kingdom is from another place."

"You are a king, then!" said Pilate.

Jesus answered, "You are right in saying I am a king. In fact, for this reason I was born, and for this I came into the world, to testify to the truth. Everyone on the side of truth listens to me."

"What is truth?" Pilate asked. With this he went out again to the Jews and said *(John 18:33-38)*, "I find no basis for a charge against this man."

But they insisted, "He stirs up the people all over Judea by his teaching. He started in Galilee and has come all the way here."

On hearing this, Pilate asked if the man was a Galilean. When he learned that Jesus was under Herod's jurisdiction, he sent him to Herod, who was also in Jerusalem at that time. . . .

Pilate called together the chief priests, the rulers and the people, and said to them, "You brought me this man as one who was inciting the people to rebellion. I have examined him in your presence and have found no basis for your charges against him. Neither has Herod, for he sent him back to us; as you can see, he has done nothing to deserve death" *(Luke 23:4-7, 13-15)*. "But it is your custom for me to release to you one prisoner at the time of the Passover. Do you want me to release 'the king of the Jews'?" *(John 18:39)*.

For he knew it was out of envy that they had handed Jesus over to him.

While Pilate was sitting on the judge's seat, his wife sent him this message: "Don't have anything to do with that innocent man, for I have suffered a great deal today in a dream because of him" *(Matt. 27:18-19)*.

They shouted back, "No, not him! Give us Barabbas!" Now Barabbas had taken part in a rebellion.

Then Pilate took Jesus and had him flogged. The soldiers twisted together a crown of thorns and put it on his head. They clothed him in a purple robe and went up to him again and again, saying, "Hail, king of the Jews!" And they struck him in the face.

Once more Pilate came out and said to the Jews, "Look, I am bringing him out to you to let you know that I find no basis for a charge against him." When Jesus came out wearing the crown of thorns and the purple robe, Pilate said to them, "Here is the man!" (John 18:40—19:5).

"What shall I do, then, with Jesus who is called Christ?" Pilate asked.

They all answered, "Crucify him!"

"Why? What crime has he committed?" asked Pilate (Matt. 27:22-23). "I have found in him no grounds for the death penalty. Therefore I will have him punished and then release him" (Luke 23:22).

But they shouted all the louder, "Crucify him!" (Matt. 27:23).

The Jews insisted, "We have a law, and according to that law he must die, because he claimed to be the Son of God."

When Pilate heard this, he was even more afraid, and he went back inside the palace. "Where do you come from?" he asked Jesus, but Jesus gave him no answer. "Do you refuse to speak to me?" Pilate asked. "Don't you realize I have power either to free you or to crucify you?"

Jesus answered, "You would have no power over me if it were not given to you from above. Therefore the one who handed me over to you is guilty of a greater sin."

From then on, Pilate tried to set Jesus free, but the Jews kept shouting, "If you let this man go, you are no friend of Caesar. Anyone who claims to be a king opposes Caesar."

When Pilate heard this, he brought Jesus out and sat down on the judge's seat . . . "Here is your king," Pilate said to the Jews.

But they shouted, "Take him away! Take him away! Crucify him!"

"Shall I crucify your king?" Pilate asked.

"We have no king but Caesar," the chief priests answered *(John 19:7-15)*.

When Pilate saw that he was getting nowhere, but that instead an uproar was starting, he took water and washed his hands in front of the crowd. "I am innocent of this man's blood," he said. "It is your responsibility!"

All the people answered, "Let his blood be on us and on our children!"

Then he released Barabbas to them. But he had Jesus flogged, and *(Matt. 27:24-26)* handed him over to them to be crucified *(John 19:16)*.

With insight, English playwright William Shakespeare wrote:

> *There is a tide in the affairs of men*
> *Which, taken at the flood, leads on to fortune;*
> *Omitted, all the voyage of their life*
> *Is bound in shallows and in miseries.*
>
> —From *Julius Caesar,* Act IV, Scene 3

An old legend says that in every man's lifetime is a special five minutes. At that point, the tide has risen—to ride the crest at that moment is to be carried to safety. To hesitate is to lose that only sweep of the breakers that could carry him to his destiny.

The tide rose and fell that day when Pilate hesitated to wash his hands in front of the mob. His five minutes were gone forever as he turned his back on Jesus. While Jesus stood before Pilate, Pilate stood before God. Pilate's great opportunity came the moment he uttered the inevitable question about the inescapable Christ—"What shall I do, then, with Jesus who is called Christ?" (Matt. 27:22).

THE NATURE OF PILATE'S INEVITABLE QUESTION, "WHAT SHALL I DO WITH JESUS?"

First, Pilate's query is a personal question. No one can answer for you. Thousands of mothers would gladly give everything to decide for their children. Fathers by the multitudes would make every sacrifice to see their loved ones make this right choice. But secondhand decisions and secondhand religion are empty and worthless.

Pilate asked Jesus if He was king of the Jews. Jesus responded, "Is that your own idea, or have others suggested it to you?" (John 18:34, NEB). Is the kingship of Christ in your heart firsthand or hearsay? Are the words we sing in worship describing your relationship with Jesus or are they merely handed-down repetitions? When you yourself meet Christ and take Him for your own Savior and Lord, Jesus is no longer a topic to be stored away. He is your Friend who stimulates you to learn with the zest of personal discovery! Paul cried out, "I know whom I have believed" (2 Tim. 1:12).

John Wesley possessed only secondhand religion when he went to Georgia as a missionary to the Indians. He had not made that dynamic personal decision regarding "What shall I do with Jesus?" One day his ship was tossed about in a terrifying Atlantic storm. He was gripped by fear. However, through that storm a small group of Moravian missionaries on board displayed an inner serenity. When the storm clattered away, Wesley asked them, "Weren't you afraid?"

One of them replied, "Afraid? Why should I be afraid? I know Christ!" Looking straight at John Wesley, he asked, "Do you know Christ?"

For the first time, Wesley realized he had not made

that personal, firsthand decision to accept Jesus as Savior and Lord.

"What shall I do with Jesus?"

Second, it is a pressing question. Many questions in life can be put off—but not this one. You must answer the inevitable question about the inescapable Christ. There's no way around Him. When the curtain closes on the drama of your life, you will have answered that question one way or another. As Clarence Macartney explained, "Christ is . . . not an ideal, not an example to be vaguely followed . . . He is a choice, a decision, and we vote for Him or against Him!"[1]

During Easter season many years ago, an art gallery in London displayed several paintings of events occurring during the week of Jesus' crucifixion. One of the paintings was appropriately named "Christ Before Pilate."

People stood silently before the painting, catching its mood and message. A little girl stared at the scene. Finally, she could keep quiet no longer and cried out, "Will no one come to help Jesus?"

That little girl was Evangeline Booth. When she grew up, she spent her life helping Jesus reach others. She followed her father as the chief of the Salvation Army around the world—a ministry that continues the work of saving and healing that Jesus began!

With urgency, you must ask, "What will I do with Jesus?"

Third, it is a present question. Before this hour is up you will have given an answer. There's no middle ground. You cannot avoid deciding for or against Jesus. Though Christ does not force himself on you, His Spirit pleads with you, presses His claims of Lordship in your life, and presents His love to you. Jesus forces no one into His kingdom. But He puts himself squarely before you, demanding a decision! You are free to choose, but you are not free to avoid choosing.

PILATE'S ATTEMPTS TO DEAL WITH THE INEVITABLE QUESTION, "WHAT SHALL I DO WITH JESUS?"

First, Pilate tried to ignore Jesus. As quickly as possible, he attempted to hand Jesus back to the Jews. He didn't want to be troubled with the Nazarene. Wishing to remain uninvolved, Pilate tried to dispense with Him.

Pilate is so much like the man who said: "I don't go to church for three reasons: First, God doesn't make me go. Second, there's a big difference between what I am and what I should be. And third, I don't want to be reminded about it."

We may ignore Jesus—but we shall not escape Him. We cannot escape Jesus by ignoring Him any more than we can escape dying by ignoring death.[2] Jesus stands at the crossroads of life, and all of us pass by and make our choice.

Second, Pilate tried to take Jesus lightly. Realizing the issue would not go away, he made jest of the whole thing. Jesus was accused of claiming to be king, so Pilate was forced to handle the case. But "He did not take anything seriously . . . He was never impressed with their charges against Jesus. But he did not go into it deeply. It was a routine disturbance, and nothing to get stirred up about . . . His chief concern was to get it over somehow . . . Pilate's position was: 'Let the innocent Man go, if possible and convenient.' But the main thing was to be done with it. It was a nuisance . . . end it one way . . . [or] another."[3]

Looking at Jesus—a king in rags, deserted by His followers, a helpless victim of priests, clothed in mock coronation robes—Pilate asks, "Are you the king of the Jews?" (John 18:33). But he never took Jesus' kingship seriously!

How about you? Have you given serious thought about what to say when God asks: "What have you done with Jesus?"

Third, Pilate tried to patronize Jesus. At least three times he announced, "I find no fault in this man." He believed Jesus to be innocent. He insisted that Jesus was a good man, but he failed to recognize Jesus' uniqueness as the Son of God. Thus, Pilate was never deeply moved about Jesus.

"We can patronize [Jesus] . . . We can insist that He was a very good Man, an interesting [Person], who said some very good things, particularly the [popular] Golden Rule . . . And we can speak of it all just as we would praise a drawing made by a six-year-old child. We approve it, and that is the end of the matter."[4] Are you deeply moved by God's unique demonstration of His love through Jesus Christ?

Fourth, Pilate tried to compromise Jesus! After getting to know Jesus face-to-face in private, Pilate took more interest in the outcome. John noted, "From then on, Pilate tried to set Jesus free" (John 19:12). He made renewed efforts to release Him. But each effort was softened by compromising with Jesus' enemies. His private, personal desire to do something constructive for Jesus was lost in his compromises. Pilate could have set Jesus free, but he compromised on Barabbas. Believing Jesus innocent of all crime, Pilate compromised by having Jesus beaten. Though he didn't personally crack the whip or spit on Jesus, he allowed it to happen. He thought himself neutral, and he did nothing. Indecision is the worst of all decisions.

If you haven't crowned Jesus Lord of your life, what compromises are you making? What has become more important to you than Christ?

Fifth, Pilate tried to evade responsibility for Jesus. He brought in a wash basin and made a little ceremony to remove personal responsibility for Jesus—a kind of baptism into irresponsibility. He tried to wash his hands of the whole affair. Vainly he washed and exclaimed, "I am innocent of this man's blood . . . It is your responsibility" (Matt. 27:24). It may have cleansed his hands, but it didn't cleanse his conscience.

William Edward Biederwolf depicted a scene in his book *Letters from Hell.* A stream runs through the lost world. A man kneels beside it washing his hands. He is slumped over with despair, for he has washed his hands long and hard, but with no success. Someone touches his shoulder and asks, "Pilate, what are you doing?"

He lifts his hands, as red as the blood of Jesus, and utters a shriek that echoes through the corridors: "Will they never be clean? Will they never be clean?"[5]

Poor Pilate—they never will—never!

"Life is not made for neutrals."[6] Life does not present us with three choices—for, against, or indifferent—but with two choices, for or against, one or the other. When Jesus said, "He who is not with me is against me" (Luke 11:23), He stated a fact for people like Pilate who try to wash their hands of spiritual responsibility.[7] Water can't wash away the crimson stain on a man's conscience. Ceremonies don't bring cleansing. Only God can do that!

THE OUTCOME OF PILATE'S ANSWER TO THE INEVITABLE QUESTION, "WHAT SHALL I DO WITH JESUS?"

Pilate turned away from Jesus and consented to His crucifixion. Having been warned by his own sense of justice, by his conscience, and by his wife's dream, Pilate gave in to pressure. Like it or not, he crucified Jesus. "But with loud shouts they insistently demanded that he be crucified, and their shouts prevailed" (Luke 23:23). Reason didn't win. Logic didn't win. Common sense didn't win. Objective evidence didn't win. Justice didn't win. "Their shouts prevailed!" It was a sad moment for Pilate—and all of Jerusalem! Why did their yelling put pressure on Pilate?

First, Pilate buckled under the pressure of his past. His six years as governor of Judea were marked with the blood of many sins. These terrible sins of his past were suddenly thrown up to him. Haunted by his past sins and failures, he did not want them exposed to Caesar.

What will you do with Jesus? Don't crucify Him anew by hanging on to past sins. If you refuse to confess them, you decide against Jesus. However, "If we confess our sins, he is faithful and just and will forgive us our sins and purify us from all unrighteousness" (1 John 1:9).

Second, Pilate buckled under the pressure of his peers. Here is one of the saddest verses in the Bible: "Wanting to satisfy the crowd, Pilate . . . handed him over to be crucified" (Mark 15:15). It's a sad day when we allow peer pressure to rob us of our good judgment and clear conscience.

For Pilate, the most important thing was the approval of the crowd. His sense of morality fluctuated with the polls. Instead of accepting his personal responsibility, Pilate followed the poll of public opinion. He wanted to be acceptable in the eyes of the crowd. Instead of being a voice, he became an echo. He tragically demonstrated the danger of making public opinion the deciding factor. When he should have asked, "What is the right thing to do?" he wondered, "What will please most of the people?" The number one question is not "What are people saying?" but "What has God said?"

Consider jaywalking. Do you watch the light and follow its instruction or step out into the street with those who choose to cross regardless of the signal?

Are you getting your signals from God or from people? Are you breaking God's law to keep in step with everyone else in your crowd?

Regardless of what people think or do or say, you must face the inevitable question about the inescapable Christ: "What will you do with Jesus?"

Third, Pilate buckled under the pressure of his position. When the mob threatened, "If you let this man go, you are no friend of Caesar" (John 19:12), Pilate feared for his job, his position of prestige. He sold out Jesus in order to keep his spot in the political limelight. But poor Pilate—in a few months his royal robes would grace the back of another. His scepter of authority would be caressed by another hand! According to history, Pilate was soon recalled to Rome to answer charges for misconduct in public office. He escaped trial only because Emperor Tiberius died before Pilate arrived in Rome. Stripped of power, Pilate vanished from public view. He lost everything he attempted to save. He crucified Jesus to save himself—but he lost everything for which he had sacrificed Jesus! He gave up so much for so little!

An ancient king was so tormented by thirst during a battle that he offered his kingdom to his enemies if they would permit him a drink of water. When he finished his long, cool drink, he exclaimed, "Ah, wretched me, who for such a momentary gratification have lost so great a kingdom!"

Many people sell themselves short by giving into pressures of past sins, the pressures of people's opinions, the pressures of positions of prestige—all so fleeting. Jesus alone can meet the needs of your heart.

Jesus stands before us. What are we going to do with Jesus? The crowd shouted, "Crucify him!" Pilate followed the line of least resistance. We crucify Him anew if we turn aside His invitation to come and find peace with God through Jesus Christ. You either crucify Him or crown Him Lord of your life. The throne in your heart will not remain empty! If you remain on it, you order Jesus crucified: "Away with Him!" If you let Him nail your sins to the Cross, you open the way for Jesus to occupy your heart's throne. Only Jesus can "welcome, pardon, cleanse, relieve!" You need Jesus. You need Him in life. You need Him in death. You need Him at the judgment—for, in the final analysis, *you* are on trial, not Jesus! All He asks is that you will trust Him—honestly and completely.

> Crown Him or crucify Him . . . Love Him or leave Him . . . Receive Him or reject Him . . . Believe on Him or turn Him [away]. You must decide . . . Heaven bends down to catch the sound of your answer . . . The recording angel . . . has dipped his pen in the blood of Jesus and . . . holds it poised over the Book of Life. Tell me . . . will this mighty angel write [over] your name . . . "Child of God" as you come [now] accepting Christ or will he sadly shake his head and write the fearful word "lost" on your record?[8]

First, acknowledge yourself as a sinner. "All have sinned and fall short of the glory of God" (Rom. 3:23). Without Christ, you are a sinner.

Second, believe in Christ. "Believe in the Lord Jesus, and you will be saved" (Acts 16:31). If you have doubts, consider the alternatives and take Jesus at His word.

Third, confess Christ as your Savior. "If you confess with your mouth, 'Jesus is Lord,' and believe in your heart that God raised him from the dead, you will be saved" (Rom. 10:9).

Fourth, declare Christ as Lord. Jesus says, "Whoever acknowledges me before men, I will also acknowledge him before my Father in heaven" (Matt. 10:32).

Here's the inevitable question about the inescapable Christ: "What will you do with Jesus?"

> *Jesus is standing in Pilate's hall—*
> *Friendless, forsaken, betrayed by all:*
> *Hearken! What meaneth the sudden call!*
> *What will you do with Jesus?*
>
> *Will you evade Him as Pilate tried?*
> *Or will you choose Him, whate'er betide?*
> *Vainly you struggle from Him to hide:*
> *What will you do with Jesus?*

What will you do with Jesus?
Neutral you cannot be.
Some day your heart will be asking,
"What will He do with me?"

—Unknown

5

"IN MY PLACE CONDEMNED HE STOOD"

MARK 15:1-15
CF. MATTHEW 27:15-26; LUKE 23:13-25; JOHN 18:39—19:16

> Wanting to release Jesus, Pilate appealed to them again. But they kept shouting, "Crucify him! Crucify him!"
>
> For the third time he spoke to them: "Why? What crime has this man committed? I have found in him no grounds for the death penalty. Therefore I will have him punished and then release him."
>
> But with loud shouts they insistently demanded that he be crucified, and their shouts prevailed. So Pilate decided to grant their demand. He released the man who had been thrown into prison for insurrection and murder, the one they asked for, and surrendered Jesus to their will *(Luke 23:20-25)*.

It was a strange, passing moment when Jesus and Barabbas crossed paths. Their brief encounter had eternal consequences. According to very early manuscripts of Matthew's Gospel, Barabbas' name was "Jesus Barabbas." "Barabbas" is an Aramaic name that means "Son of a father." Jesus Barabbas stood before Pilate condemned, guilty of rebellion and murder. Jesus Bar-Joseph stood beside him, innocent and sinless! One would live; the other would die!

58

Edgar A. Guest caught that dramatic moment:

Barabbas, convicted of murder; Barabbas, the ne'er-do-well,

Awaiting the death of a felon, sat in his prison cell.

Already his cross was fashioned—at dawn they would nail him high;

When down through the dingy cell house there came to his ears a cry:

"Barabbas! Barabbas! Barabbas! Barabbas whose hands are red!

Take you the lowly Nazarene's and spare us his life instead."

And a sickened and frightened Pilate who dared not their pleas deny

Released to the mob Barabbas and ordered the Christ to die.

They saved him with shout and tumult, Barabbas with hands unclean,

Barabbas, of evil doing, who knew not the Nazarene,

Was saved by a sudden fancy, turned loose and not knowing why—

Sent back to the street and gutter, alone and unloved, to die.

In the gloom of that gray Good Friday the Savior they crucified,

And the mad throng stood about Him and mocked till the hour He died;

They knew not what they were doing, but Pilate, pale and afraid,

Stood at the window watching, regretting the choice they'd made![1]

The Bible doesn't tell us what happened to Barabbas after he was released, but if he followed the mob to Calvary, the thought must have burned in his heart: "That's my cross He's dying on!"

Jesus became Barabbas' substitute in guilt and death. The Bible tells the startling fact that Jesus is our substitute, our sacrifice for sin, our stand-in before moral justice. Mystery veils the Atonement! We simply do not understand completely how God does it! But faith finds the solid foundation of God's promise and provision. What happened to Barabbas happens to us spiritually as we seek God's forgiveness. One hymnwriter penned it vividly:

> *Bearing shame and scoffing rude,*
> *In my place condemned He stood—*
> *Sealed my pardon with His blood.*
> *Hallelujah! what a Saviour!*
> —Phillip P. Bliss

Three basic truths shine out of this portrayal of Barabbas—"In my place condemned He stood."

BY GOD'S JUSTICE, WE GET WHAT WE DESERVE

Without Jesus, we stand condemned before God's moral law. Barabbas represents each person born into this world. As a sinner, Barabbas, a thief and murderer, was caught and brought to justice. He was guilty and condemned. Strangely, the crowd identified with Barabbas instead of Jesus. They deliberately chose lawlessness instead of moral justice. William Barclay pointed out, "One of the New Testament words for sin is *anomia,* which means lawlessness. In the human heart is a streak that resents law, that desires to do as it likes, that wants to smash the confining barriers and kick over the traces and refuse all discipline."[2]

Looking beyond our facade, the Bible says, "There is no one righteous, not even one" (Rom. 3:10). God's Word, revealing our hearts, states, "For all have sinned and fall short of the glory of God" (v. 23). Standing alone, we are condemned for wrong living, wrong conduct, wrong attitudes, and wrong relationships. The verdict is pronounced—"Guilty!" Even our conscience agrees. When we are painfully honest, there is no one else to blame.

Roy Hession illustrated it beautifully:

> A saintly African Christian told a congregation once that, as he was climbing the hill to the meeting, he heard steps behind him. He turned and saw a Man carrying a very heavy load up the hill on His back. He was full of sympathy for Him and spoke to Him. Then he noticed that His hands were scarred, and he realized that it was Jesus.
>
> He said to Him, "Lord, are you carrying the world's sins up that hill?"
>
> "No," said the Lord Jesus, "not the *world's* sin, just *yours!*"
>
> As that African simply told the vision God had just given him, the people's hearts and his heart were broken as they saw their sins at the cross. Our hearts need to be broken, too, and only when they are shall we be willing for the confessions, the apologies, the reconciliations and the restitutions that are involved in a true repentance of sin.[3]

Let God's searchlight of truth scan your inner corridors: "Search me, O God, and know my heart; test my thoughts. Point out anything you find in me that makes you sad" (Ps. 139:23-24, TLB).

BY GOD'S MERCY, WE DON'T GET WHAT WE DESERVE

God has planned an alternative to our condemnation. Like Barabbas, we are guilty of sin. But God has effected a plan for our rescue. The Bible says, "But God demonstrates his own love for us in this: While we were still sinners, Christ died for us" (Rom. 5:8). God in His mercy has given Jesus, His own Son, as His alternative to the Barabbas in us. Of course, Barabbas is the world's alternative to Jesus. To follow his path of guilt and strife and rebellion is to discover that "the wages of sin is death, but the gift of God is eternal life through Jesus Christ our Lord" (Rom. 6:23).

God's holiness seeks justice, but God's love offers mercy. Jesus is God's great act of mercy. God's mercy provides for the atonement of our sins: "For God so loved the world that he gave his one and only Son, that whoever believes in him shall not perish but have eternal life. For God did not send his Son into the world to condemn the world, but to save the world through him" (John 3:16-17).

> *I need no other argument;*
> *I need no other plea.*
> *It is enough that Jesus died,*
> *And that He died for me.*
> —Lidie H. Edmunds

The Bible announces God's purpose in sending Jesus as our substitute: "The Son of Man did not come to be served, but to serve, and to give his life as a ransom for many" (Mark 10:45).

The Portland *Oregonian* once carried a front-page picture of a man who risked his life to rescue three small puppies that had fallen into an old, abandoned well. In spite of the possibility that the walls would cave in, the man volunteered to be lowered into the well. At great personal risk, he saved the helpless puppies.

We were helpless and hopeless in sin and guilt. Along came Jesus by God's mercy and gave His life for us. He made it possible for us to have a new beginning! Jesus is God's personal offer of mercy; we don't get what we deserve. Jesus himself took what we deserve.

A mountain school was notorious for running off teachers. The big, rough boys intimidated every teacher who was hired. The school board finally got a young, dedicated man to come. He quickly sized up the situation and announced, "Fellows, I haven't had much experience at running a school, so I want you to make up the rules of the class. I'll write them down as you agree to them."   .

As the teacher picked up his chalk, one student volunteered: "Start and stop on time."

The teacher wrote it down.

Another suggested, "Twenty-minute recesses and an hour for lunch."

The class agreed in unison. Other rules were set by the class—no stealing, no cheating, no homework. When all seemed satisfied, the teacher asked, "Now tell me what penalties you suggest for cheating and stealing."

The whole school agreed that cheating should be punished with 5 strokes of the rod and stealing with 10 strokes—both given with the offender's coat off.

Things seemed to work fine until one day a lunch was stolen from Tom, a big, husky youth. Finally, a little, frail boy in hand-me-down clothes admitted his guilt. The rules required him to be whipped with 10 strokes. Whimpering, he begged the teacher to let him keep his coat on. But the rules demanded that he remove his coat to receive the blows. The students insisted on justice—that the rules be followed.

When he reluctantly took off his coat, the class choked in silence. He had no shirt, and his skinny body looked like skin stretched over bones.

His teacher knew he couldn't whip that boy, but what could he do? Suddenly big Tom walked up, stood between the teacher and the little boy, and said, "Since it was my lunch he stole, I'll take his whipping for him, Teacher!"

The class watched as the teacher struck the blows required by justice but by mercy laid upon the one who had been wronged. When it was over, the frail lad put his hand on big Tom's arm and said through tears, "Thanks, Tom. It would have killed me!"

It *did* kill Jesus when He stepped into Barabbas' place—and ours! Isaiah anticipated it: "He was wounded for our transgressions, he was bruised for our iniquities . . . and with his stripes we are healed" (Isa. 53:5, KJV). Out of God's mercy, we don't get what we deserve!

BY GOD'S GRACE, WE GET WHAT WE DON'T DESERVE

In response to our faith, Jesus takes our place of condemnation. The apostle John wrote: "This is love: not that we loved God, but that he loved us and sent his Son as an atoning sacrifice for our sins" (1 John 4:10). Jesus, who was unworthy to die, stood in place of Barabbas, who was unworthy to live. The whole scene depicts self-giving love—one Man stretched out on another man's cross. Barabbas lived because Jesus was willing to die. Jesus did for Barabbas what He did for us. We can experience God's grace by accepting Jesus' completed work for us.

Neil Strait wrote: "For in that moment Christ took the place of Barabbas, who should have died. Christ took the place of the condemned, that through His life the condemned might live. And it is a true picture of Calvary. Christ giving life, that men with the pronouncement of death upon their souls might live."[4]

Paul urged, "Be reconciled to God. God made him who had no sin to be sin for us, so that in him we might become the righteousness of God" (2 Cor. 5:20-21).

Missionaries to China struggled with the overwhelming task of learning to read and write with the 214 symbols of Chinese "radicals," which combine uniquely into nearly 50,000 ideographs. What a formidable barrier for Westerners desiring to communicate the good news of Jesus!

One day . . . one of the missionaries . . . was studying a particular Chinese ideograph, the one which means "righteousness." He noticed that it contained an upper and lower part. The upper part was simply the Chinese symbol for a *lamb*. Directly under the lamb was a second symbol, the first-person pronoun *I*. Suddenly he discerned an amazingly well-coded message hidden within the ideograph: *I under the lamb am righteous!*

It was nothing less than the heart of the gospel he had crossed the ocean to preach! Chinese [people] were startled when he called their attention to the hidden message. They had never noticed it, but once he pointed it out, they saw it clearly. When he asked, "Which lamb must we be 'under' to be righteous?" they had no answer. With . . . delight he told them of "the Lamb that was slain from the creation of the world" (Rev. 13:8), the same "Lamb of God, who takes away the sin of the world" (John 1:29).[5]

By grace, we get what we don't deserve—the righteousness of Jesus!

A writer of fiction portrays Barabbas following the procession to the crucifixion. As he watched Jesus being nailed to the Cross, Barabbas was deeply moved with the thought: "I should have been carrying that Cross, not He! He saved me! I should have been hanging there, not He! He saved me!"

Whether true or not, it is certainly true that Barabbas was included among the sinners for whom Jesus died to save. And so were we! The Bible says, "He himself bore our sins in his body on the tree, so that we might die to sins and live for righteousness; by his wounds you have been healed" (1 Pet. 2:24).

The good news is that Jesus died, not for a faceless, anonymous crowd, but for me. If I seek His forgiveness and invite Him into my life, it was for me He died! I must let Him be my Savior.

On the East Coast, two good friends ate lunch together nearly every workday. One was a Jewish businessman; the other a Christian. Often the Christian friend shared the claims of Jesus, and his Jewish friend listened politely but never made any comment.

Suddenly one day the Jewish man was stricken physically. Word came to his friend that he was dying. Twice he tried to see his dying friend, but the physician wouldn't permit visitors. The Christian persisted.

Finally the doctor said, "Let him in. He can't do any harm now."

The friend promised not to talk. He slipped into the room, knelt beside the bed, and held his friend's hand. Silently the Christian prayed for his longtime companion. Though the sick man was breathing heavily, his eyes shut, there seemed to be a momentary change. He opened his eyes, looked at his kneeling friend, and said softly before slipping into eternity: "Not Barabbas, but this man!"

God's forgiveness is simple but profound. It is free but not cheap. While Jesus died on the Cross for Barabbas and me, I must personally invite the living Christ into my heart. Jesus said, "I stand at the door and knock. If anyone hears my voice and opens the door, I will come in" (Rev. 3:20).

A young monk in Germany named Martin Luther unburdened his troubled conscience to an elder monk in the cloister. Finally the old man asked, "Do you believe in the forgiveness of sins?"

Luther replied, "Yes, of course! I confess it daily in the Creed."

His wise counselor said, "But you do not really believe it. You believe in the forgiveness of sins for David and Peter and the thief on the cross. But you do not believe in the forgiveness of sins for yourself. You will not find peace until you can say, 'I believe in the forgiveness of *my* sins.'"

I will not enjoy God's mercy and love until the crucified Christ brings me to a personal acceptance of His forgiveness. "In my place condemned He stood."

Jesus took my marred and spotted record and died, and in God's sight it was buried with Him in the tomb. And He gave me His unblemished record and His righteousness. Again, I am under the Lamb! I get what I don't deserve—that's grace! "In my place condemned He stood."

> *Upon the cross of Jesus*
> *Mine eyes at times can see*
> *The very dying form of One*
> *Who suffered there for me.*

And from my smitten heart, with tears,
These wonders I confess:
The wonders of His glorious love,
And my own unworthiness.
—Elizabeth C. Clephane

6

MOCKERY OF THE MASTER

MARK 15:16-20
CF. MATTHEW 27:27-31

The soldiers led Jesus away into the palace (that is, the Praetorium) and called together the whole company of soldiers. They put a purple robe on him, then twisted together a crown of thorns and set it on him. And they began to call out to him, "Hail, king of the Jews!" Again and again they struck him on the head with a staff and spit on him. Falling on their knees, they paid homage to him. And when they had mocked him, they took off the purple robe and put his own clothes on him. Then they led him out to crucify him *(Mark 15:16-20)*.

My two traveling companions and I entered the Tower of London. After walking through St. James Cathedral, the ancient coronation place of English kings and queens, we stood in a line that filed through the building that housed the crown jewels and treasures of the British Empire. In all of my life, I have never seen such displayed wealth—gold and silver, jewels and exquisite serving sets, candelabra and royal coats of arms.

Under heavy guard, the line weaved its way down into a basement-level room that is really a huge vault with mechanical vault-doors weighing several tons. In that protected vault, two lines of people circled a huge glass encasement that occupied the center of the room. We saw crowns that have rested on the heads of monarchs of the empire. We saw the jewel-bedecked scepters signifying authority. We saw the royal purple and scarlet robes trimmed with gold that cloaked royal wardrobes. A hush fell as the spectators gazed in awe at the trappings of earthly kingdoms.

Another scene catches my imagination with vivid contrasts. Its trappings were crude and cruel: a purple robe, a crown of thorns, a scepter of papyrus reed! There was no hush of reverence! The room echoed with coarse laughter from obnoxious men, hardened by bloodshed and made insensitive to human suffering. Vulgarity and blasphemy oozed from their lips, revealing inner character. This was no coronation ceremony—it was a joke!

At the hands of these brutal soldiers, Jesus suffered a cruel mockery: "Hail, king of the Jews!" (Mark 15:18). With jest, they teased Jesus like a cat teases a mouse before killing it. Over the bleeding back of Jesus, they hung a makeshift purple robe as a pretense of His kingship. The thorny crown was woven cautiously and given roughly without any intent to offer allegiance. Proclamations from their lips wreaked with insincerity and hypocrisy. Clumsily, they fashioned a king to their own liking! With the depths of contempt, they spit on Jesus again and again. After bowing their knees before Jesus in mock loyalty, the soldiers stripped the Master of His purple robe, put His torn rags back on Him, and led Him to be crucified! Pilate's bodyguards had had their sadistic fun in the courtyard of Antonio's Fortress—now the silly joke was over.

However, after mocking Jesus, they may have had some second thoughts in quieter moments—what a contrast! Peter wrote, "When they hurled their insults at him, he did not retaliate; when he suffered, he made no threats" (1 Pet. 2:23). But for Jesus, the joke is not over! People still mock Him today.

THE MOCKERY THAT SPRINGS FROM IGNORANCE

Those Roman soldiers didn't have much exposure to a faith in our Heavenly Father. They knew nothing of a Messiah. Those men simply scorned Jesus for what they thought was weakness and failure. Their deeds of cruelty to Jesus were done basically in ignorance. To them, Jesus was just another "deluded Galilean going to a cross."

According to Philo, the same kind of treatment was given by a mob to a young imbecile boy in Alexandria. It was not uncommon mockery to people deemed crazy.

Yet even today there is a mockery through ignorance of the real Jesus. Nominal Christians have painted such a caricature of Jesus that He is often regarded as nonsense by people who do not understand. People make fun of whatever they do not understand. Since Jesus goes cross-current to the thinking and conduct of our world, He becomes the target of mockery by the uninformed.

Pilate could find no fault in Jesus, and neither can our world. He stands there in His purity, His openness, His goodness—and people filled with sin, guilt, and shame react by ridiculing virtue and innocence—something they themselves do not possess. An ill will is directed toward the person of Christ because He is *not* inferior; therefore, people make light of that which is beyond their reach!

Out of ignorance, many people do not know that Jesus and His gift of eternal life are *not* beyond reach. The Master reaches out for each one of us.

THE MOCKERY THAT SPRINGS FROM HYPOCRISY

Peeking through the gateway, you would have seen soldiers kneeling down on the cobblestones in the ancient posture of showing respect and loyalty. You would have heard them giggling in sonorous tones, "Hail, king of the Jews!" Outwardly they had the appearance of homage—but it was really mockery.

That band of Roman guards had bestowed on Jesus all the trimmings of royalty, but without power. They gave all the gestures of homage, but without reality. Their feigned discipleship to Jesus was a burlesque of allegiance.

People still mock and wound Jesus when they offer Him only a nominal homage and give lip service without heart. Though they say they are Christians, they have not the Spirit of Christ. Paul told Timothy some of the signs of the last days: "People will be lovers of themselves, lovers of money, boastful, proud, abusive, disobedient to their parents, ungrateful, unholy, without love, unforgiving, slanderous, without self-control, brutal, not lovers of the good, treacherous, rash, conceited, lovers of pleasure rather than lovers of God—having a form of godliness but denying its power" (2 Tim. 3:2-5).

Anyone can look like a Christian. Anyone can speak the right words. Any old sinner can announce, "Jesus is Lord." But Jesus speaks to people who mock Him through hypocrisy: "Why do you call me, 'Lord, Lord,' and do not do what I say?" (Luke 6:46).

Someday God will separate the wheat and the weeds, the sheep and the goats, the real followers of Jesus and the phonies! People may mock Jesus now by going through the religious motions, but they can't fool Him!

Once upon a time there was a diamond ring—well, it *looked* like a diamond ring. Everybody *thought* it was a diamond—except the jeweler. He said, "Diamonds and glass may be made of the same stuff to start with, but they sure turn out differently. I can tell them apart because the diamond is transformed. It's got sparkle like nothing else! And strength and endurance—and a price tag like nothing else too!"

Once upon a time there was a Christian—well, he *looked* like a Christian. Everybody *thought* he was a Christian—except God. Christians and unbelievers are the same to start with—all sinners! But they certainly turn out differently. God can tell them apart, because the Christian is transformed. He has sparkle like no one else! And God's strength and endurance are his! The price was high—it cost the life of God's own Son, Jesus Christ. He died for you and me.

To end the mockery and become the real prize, confess your sins, and ask Jesus Christ into your heart and life. He will transform that old nature into His new nature! He'll make you a real Christian, with sparkle on the inside. You can become His purchased, prized possession forever!

THE MOCKERY THAT SPRINGS FROM INDIFFERENCE

Why would those soldiers care about a Jew called Jesus? He mattered little to them! They dressed Jesus up in mock royal garb, decked Him out in the trimmings of Rome, and added the sport of mock reverence. They simply didn't care!

Since then, Jesus has been dressed up in so many ways that do not fit Him and His character. Jesus has been disguised by people who are indifferent to His claims that we must all be born again. His Lordship in the believer's life has been smothered with indifference. Somewhere through all the pantomime of religion, it was lost that Jesus is the Friend of sinners—that Jesus actually came to seek and rescue even the worst among us.

Reginald E. O. White noted, "This is the saddest irony of history, that He who came farthest to meet with us, stepping down from glory to walk with men their homeward journey to an evening rest, should walk unknown, unrecognized, and, far too frequently, unwelcome."[1]

In spite of all the cruelty heaped on Jesus by the Roman soldiers, nothing strikes a greater blow or hurls a more stinging insult than Jesus being treated as if He does not matter. Indifference wounds the heart of God!

There's a certain fatal note in the mockery of indifference. For example, a godly family can have deep and significant religious beliefs and strong convictions concerning Christian conduct. However, with a softening of convictions, the sons and daughters take a more tolerant approach. Tolerance gives way to apathy, and the third generation suffers from indifference. One fellow described the shift: "The first generation believed the creed, the second generation doubted it, and the third generation has never read it."

During a service in one of Philadelphia's gospel missions, a famous lawyer stood and described the series of events that led him to become a Christian. When he was 24 years of age, he married a beautiful, talented Christian girl. He was indifferent, a kind of practical atheist. Apathy affected his attitude toward the Lord, the Bible, and the Church. His wife kept right on, becoming more devout in spite of his efforts to break her Christian faith.

After a few years, a baby daughter was born into their home. When she was a child, the mother took her to Sunday School and church. She tried to teach her blue-eyed daughter the ways of God.

As the daughter became a beautiful young woman, her father began pulling her away from spiritual moorings. He took her to his clubs, yacht parties, dances, nightclubs—he was very proud of his daughter. On Sunday morning he would chuckle to himself as he listened to his wife begging the girl, "Doris, please get up and come with me to Sunday School and church this morning!"

His daughter would answer, "Mama, Daddy brought me in so late last night. I am so tired. Forgive me this time, Mama. I'll go with you next Sunday." Of course, next Sunday it was the same sad story.

Months and years passed—and tragedy came. The doctor told the man that his daughter was dying. There was nothing else they could do for her. He walked into her room and sat down heavily in the chair beside her bed. It was nearly an hour before he could get the courage to tell her the fatal news—and she broke into tears.

"Daddy," she sobbed. "I don't want to die! Daddy, I'm not ready to die. You've got lots of money. Isn't there anything you can do?"

The stricken parents had to restrain her in bed. When she finally calmed down, she began to ask questions and make preparations. The climax came when she turned to her father, sitting with his head in his hands, and said, "Daddy, before I go there is one question I must ask. Please tell me the truth."

"Go ahead, Darling—I'll do my best to answer you," he said.

"Daddy, you've been saying all this time not to worry too much about religion. You've been saying that if I am a good girl, live right, follow the dictates of my conscience, heaven would take care of itself. Mama has been telling me all these years that if I wanted to be with God when I died, I would have to take Jesus Christ as Savior now. Daddy, now that I am dying, please tell me: whose way shall I take, yours or Mama's?"

The lawyer leaned over her bed, picked up his daughter in his arms, and held her tight. "Darling, if you have a moment to spare, take Mother's way!"

Before he lowered her back onto the bed, she was dead. As he stood testifying in that gospel mission in deep agony, he said with emotion, "Brothers and sisters, only God knows whether my darling girl had time enough to take Mother's way."[2]

There is no time to waste in mockery of Jesus' way through ignorance, hypocrisy, or indifference. The Bible urges, "Now is the time of God's favor, now is the day of salvation" (2 Cor. 6:2). "How shall we escape if we ignore such a great salvation?" (Heb. 2:3). Examine yourself and your lifestyle and your loyalties. Make sure you are not mocking Jesus by your life and your attitudes and your lack of commitment: "Jesus died for me and I don't care."

The crown, the robe, the scepter of mockery—reminders that God has ordained that some day soon "at the name of Jesus every knee should bow . . . and every tongue confess that Jesus Christ is Lord, to the glory of God the Father" (Phil. 2:10-11). He will be crowned King of Kings and Lord of Lords! Don't miss it! Bow before Him even now and let Him ascend to the throne of your heart!

7

TAKE UP THY CROSS!

MARK 15:21
CF. MATTHEW 27:32; LUKE 23:26

> A certain man from Cyrene, Simon, the father of Alexander and Rufus, was passing by on his way in from the country, and they forced him to carry the cross *(Mark 15:21)*.

Having mocked and teased Jesus, the Roman soldiers marched Him out into the streets. Though Jesus had been beaten severely, they forced Him to carry His own heavy cross—the instrument of His death. Condemned prisoners sometimes were compelled to drag the whole cross; other times they were lashed to the heavy crossbar and carried it through the streets. The soldiers always took the long way through the city's streets for everyone to see—an intended deterrent to lawlessness. Around the criminal's neck hung a placard with the man's crime inscribed—the reason for his execution.

On this day, a detail of Roman soldiers guided the gruesome procession through the crowded cobblestone streets. They never hesitated to whip Jesus as He faltered along the way.

Suddenly, Jesus' strength gave out. He couldn't bear the weight of His heavy cross any longer. His tortured body no longer responded to the stinging lashes that vainly coaxed Him on. The procession halted at the intersection where a certain man had arrived through the city gates. He had come to Jerusalem from the distant seaport of Cyrene in north Africa, known today as Tripoli. A Greek city, Cyrene had encouraged Jewish settlement. In fact, their Jewish population was one of the four main classes of citizens. Like most Jews of the Mediterranean world, at least one pilgrimage to Jerusalem to celebrate Passover was expected—and anxiously awaited.

Simon had finally arrived for the great Jewish festival. Before him was a sorry sight—a man exhausted from torture, being led outside the gates for execution.

The captain of the guard, stepping up to Simon, touched his shoulder with the flat of his spear. Without a word, Simon understood. Roman law had specified that anyone in the Roman Empire could be "compelled" to carry or assist in carrying postal packets or packages for one mile. Every person was obliged to obey this law of conscription. One moment Simon the tourist was a spectator; the next moment he was part of that strange pageantry of history—carrying another man's cross.

Three things in this brief encounter can help each Christian today in his or her walk with Jesus.

THE RECEPTION OF JESUS' CROSS

Other persons placed the cross of Jesus on Simon. Luke told it this way: "As they led him away, they seized Simon from Cyrene, who was on his way in from the country, and put the cross on him and made him carry it behind Jesus" (Luke 23:26). Sometimes other people force you who stand near Jesus to bear a heavy cross. Though you are considerate and loving, some people may single you out and make life difficult.

Circumstances of life sometimes force you to suffer for Jesus' sake. At work or school or even at home, you may be getting along minding your own business, but something can happen. Suddenly you feel the weight of Jesus' cross. Millions of people along some lonely Via Dolorosa have been compelled to bow beneath heavy burdens that were not of their own making. One fellow said, "I was forced into carrying the cross I would have refused or left on the ground!" But remember:

God hath not promised skies always blue,
Flower-strewn pathways all our lives through;
God hath not promised sun without rain,
Joy without sorrow, peace without pain.

God hath not promised we shall not know
Toil and temptation, trouble and woe;
He hath not told us we shall not bear
Many a burden, many a care.

But God hath promised strength for the day,
Rest for the labor, light for the way,
Grace for the trials, help from above,
Unfailing sympathy, undying love.*

—Annie Johnson Flint

It is Jesus' cross we are to bear, not one of our own making. Simon didn't ask for Jesus' cross, nor did he invent one to carry. Under the guise of piety, many people have taken great pains to suffer in public view—or have allowed themselves to suffer in silence as a substitute for simple, childlike faith in God's grace. Some sick souls, frustrated with insecurity, think burden-bearing earns them entrance into heaven instead of trusting in only what Christ can do!

A UPI news release from Barrio San Pedro, Philippines, told this item from several years ago:

A reformed hoodlum had himself nailed on a wooden cross today, fulfilling a wish to reenact the crucifixion of Jesus and thus atone for his sins.

Juanito Piring, 32, was nailed in each hand and tied at the feet to the 10-foot-high cross, which was erected for about 30 seconds.

Thousands of people watched from the barren field in this village 50 miles north of Manila . . .

Piring wore a loin cloth and a crown of thorns and said he had performed the act each year for five years.

Penitents in the Philippines . . . undergo bloody ordeals each year for past sins, real or imagined.

Poor Juanito did to himself physically what many untrusting Christians do emotionally all the time! The cross we should bear is not the aches or inconveniences from bad health, bad habits, or bad management of time and talent. The cross we are to bear is suffering that comes because we are identified with Jesus.

Jesus taught His disciples, "Blessed are those who are persecuted because of righteousness, for theirs is the kingdom of heaven. Blessed are you when people insult you, persecute you and falsely say all kinds of evil against you because of me. Rejoice and be glad, because great is your reward in heaven" (Matt. 5:10-12).

THE REACTIONS TO BEARING JESUS' CROSS

Simon's reactions to bearing Jesus' cross are deciphered in the historic moment and in human nature. Since we know the setting, the existing hatred between Jews and Romans, the interracial tensions, and the shame of crucifixion, we can reflect on Simon's reactions to being forced to carry Jesus' cross.

First, I believe there was a sense of frustration and disappointment. Simon, like most Jews then, had probably saved for a lifetime for this one great pilgrimage to Jerusalem to eat a Passover feast in the Holy City. It was to be a dream come true. This cherished moment turned into a nightmare as he found himself carrying a horrible cross to Golgotha.

At times, the disciple of Jesus may find himself frustrated by broken dreams—but discipleship never comes cheap and easy. The neglect of cross-bearing is apparent to a world that wishes to bury the Christian faith.

Second, I believe there was an embarrassment to Simon for being identified with Jesus. Through the jeering crowd rollicking with laughter and scorn, Simon bore Jesus' cross, following the staggering steps of the Son of God. That placard carried the written accusation of Jesus—but now Simon was identified with His disgrace.

People shun identifying with godliness. They shrink back from even the word "saint," which identified early Christians with their Jesus. Fads and fashions of our crazy world demand that even the righteous appear unrighteous—or be out of style and out of step.

Are you willing to be a "characteristic of Christ" Christian—in your world?

Third, I believe there was a deep resentment in Simon for being singled out and forced by unloving people to carry Jesus' cross. The Romans hated the Jews, and the Jews held nothing but contempt for the Roman conquerors. At the moment, surely Simon must have bitterly resented it.

Haven't you had the same experience in your world? Haven't there been times or places that unloving people have scorned your faith, laughed at your Christian morality, jeered at your identity with the wholesomeness and purity of godly living? Perhaps your first reaction has been bitterness—but put that on the cross too. There is a loneliness in a person's heart who is singled out because he goes with Jesus.

As one noted, "Always remember: you cannot carry a cross in company. Though a man were surrounded by a vast crowd, his cross is his alone and his carrying of it marks him as a man apart. Society has turned against him; otherwise, he would have no cross. No one is a friend to the man with a cross. 'They all forsook Him, and fled.'"[1]

Fourth, I believe there came later a time of healing

and reflection when Simon realized he had given special ministry to Jesus while others had fled. From Jesus' arrest in Gethsemane to His death, none of Jesus' men helped Him. This unknown Simon broke the loneliness and shared Jesus' load. Simon rendered the service of bearing Jesus' cross, and the Synoptic Gospels have preserved his name in history—Simon of Cyrene. Perhaps we have only two ways open to us: either we help crucify Jesus or we help carry His cross.

Paul puts our cross-bearing in eternal perspective: "Now if we are [God's] children, then we are heirs—heirs of God and co-heirs with Christ, if indeed we share in his sufferings in order that we may also share in his glory. I consider that our present sufferings are not worth comparing with the glory that will be revealed in us" (Rom. 8:17-18).

THE RESULTS OF BEARING JESUS' CROSS

William McCumber wrote, "Simon of Cyrene was *compelled to bear His cross,* and learned that some of life's compulsions are enriching."[2] We are all called on to bear crosses one way or another. However, the spirit in which we bear the cross determines whether it becomes an agony or a glory.

Mark makes an interesting note of this incident: "A certain man from Cyrene, Simon, the father of Alexander and Rufus" (Mark 15:21). A man is not usually identified by his sons unless they are well known to the readers. Mark's Gospel was written to the church at Rome. He must have thought the Christians at Rome knew Alexander and Rufus. When Paul concluded his letter to the church at Rome, he sent greetings: 'Greet Rufus, chosen in the Lord, and his mother, who has been a mother to me, too" (Rom. 16:13). Simon's wife had had a great influence upon the young apostle Paul.

Apparently one of the results of Simon's carrying Jesus' cross was a tremendous impact on his homelife. At some point, Simon must have become a follower of Jesus and led his boys to trust in the Christ whose cross he bore. Barclay said, "It may well be that as he looked on Jesus, Simon's bitterness turned to wondering amazement and finally to faith; that he became a Christian; and that his family became some of the choicest souls in the Roman Church . . . In the thing that seemed to be his shame he found his Saviour."[3] Perhaps Simon's most embarrassing moment became, later, the source of honor in the eyes of his sons—their father had carried the cross of Jesus!

Another result of Simon's carrying Jesus' cross was the impact on the Christian community. Many Bible scholars identify Simon as the Simeon in Acts 13:1. He was listed among the prophets and teachers in the church at Antioch. It was that group to whom the Holy Spirit said, "Set apart for me Barnabas and Saul for the work to which I have called them" (Acts 13:2). These godly men put their hands on Barnabas and Saul, prayed for them, and sent them off on the great missionary journeys that ultimately sent the good news of Jesus around the world.

In the annals of Early Church history is a tradition that Rufus became a bishop in Spain and that Alexander suffered martyrdom for his faith in Christ. Who can trace the great effects on the Christian community from that solitary act of bearing Jesus' cross?

One man, obedient to the Holy Spirit, can have a significant impact on others. General Gordon refused to become the head of state in the Belgian Congo. He refused the position as viceroy of India under British rule—all because he heard Jesus calling, "Follow Me." Gordon gave himself to help the people of Khartoum and Sudan for Jesus' sake. On his monument erected in Khartoum are these words:

This man was not great by royal state,
By sharp sword or knowledge of earth's wonder,
But more than all his race,

He saw life face to face,
And heard the still small voice of God
Above its thunder.

Certainly there was a great effect on Simon's inner life as a result of carrying Jesus' cross. To bear it, he had to lay his own burden down at the feet of Jesus. He could not have borne his own heavy load and carried Jesus' cross too. You can't effectively bear Jesus' cross until you lay your burdens at His feet.

E. Stanley Jones went into a church in India to pray. While he was meditating, it seemed a voice asked: "Are you ready for the work to which I have called you?"

"No, Lord," he replied. "I'm finished. I've reached the end of my resources. I just can't go on."

The voice said, "If you will turn the problem over to Me and not worry about it, I will take care of it."

"Lord," Dr. Jones said, "I close the bargain right here." When he got up from his knees, he had experienced the healing touch of God.[4]

A woman went alone to a place of retreat. She had spent herself in service for the Lord until she was worn down. Coming across a tiny prayer chapel, she entered its quiet room. She sat gazing out the window across a beautiful valley—then noticed the words inscribed above the window: "Cast Thy Burden upon the Lord."

Praying and meditating, she loaded all her pressures upon God and was grateful for that sense of release. Getting up to leave, she stooped to exit through the low doorway—and she saw these words inscribed overhead: "Take Up Thy Cross."

"Cast Thy Burden upon the Lord." "Take Up Thy Cross." We must learn to do them both—in that order.

To carry Jesus' cross, Simon drew near to Jesus. If he had not come near Jesus, Simon might have gone his way or been lost in the crowd. Being forced to carry the Cross brought Simon closer to Jesus.

Whatever cross you are called upon to bear, it will bring you closer to Jesus. One man said, "The cross of Christ is the sweetest burden I ever bore."

To carry Jesus' cross kept Simon walking in Jesus' footsteps. Jesus staggered along in front, led by the soldiers, bearing the inscription of His crimes. Simon plodded along behind Jesus, carrying the Cross, going where Jesus went, stepping where Jesus had already been! Jesus goes before us, bearing the reproach of our sins, and we must follow, bearing whatever shame and reproach falls on us for identifying with Christ.

The Cross keeps us in the way of our Lord. He never calls us to go alone; He goes before us and with us every step of the way. Perhaps it is that Cross that keeps us from slipping away so easily from our holy walk with Him. The songwriter exclaimed,

> *If Jesus goes with me, I'll go anywhere!*
> *'Tis heaven to me, where'er I may be,*
> *If He is there!*
> *I count it a privilege here His cross to bear.*
> *If Jesus goes with me, I'll go anywhere!*
> —C. Austin Miles

To carry Jesus' cross made Simon a partner with Jesus. Historically, Simon was linked with Jesus' great work. Simon couldn't destroy sin and death with Jesus, but he did help Jesus' weakness in the flesh. Simon didn't die on the Cross for our atonement, but he assisted our Christ in the moment of His ministry of reconciliation.

We can't participate in Jesus' passion at the Cross, but we can share with Him in His compassion for lost people. We can't purchase freedom for people bound in habits and sin, but we can tell them of one who has lived to set them free! Whatever cross we are called to bear, it is an expression of our unity in Christ. We are His colaborers!

Paul said, "I have been crucified with Christ and I no longer live, but Christ lives in me. The life I live in the body, I live by faith in the Son of God, who loved me and gave himself for me" (Gal. 2:20).

To carry Jesus' cross brought the smile of Jesus. God's approval rests on those who follow Christ and take up their cross! Knowing Jesus' character, I'm sure He gave a smile to Simon—and Simon never forgot it. With a twinkle in God's eyes, we hear the words: "Blessed is the man that endureth temptation: for when he is tried, he shall receive the crown of life, which the Lord hath promised to them that love Him" (James 1:12, KJV).

An American businessman went to Oberammergau, Germany, to see the famous passion play depicting the story of the Cross. At the conclusion of the drama, the businessman went onstage to meet Anton Lang, who played the role of the Christ. Having bought an expensive camera, he eagerly took pictures of the staging area—even snapping a picture of Anton Lang still dressed in costume—but much to Mr. Lang's displeasure.

Looking for something of interest, he noticed the big cross Mr. Lang had carried up the hill to Calvary. Quickly turning to his wife, he said, "Take my camera. I'm going to lift up the cross. When I get it on my shoulder, snap my picture carrying the cross. That would be a novel picture for our friends back home."

Noticing that Mr. Lang was frowning at the irreverence, the businessman said, "Oh, you don't mind, do you, Mr. Lang?" Before Mr. Lang could protest, he stooped to lift the cross to his shoulder—but he couldn't budge it off the floor. The cross was made of heavy iron-oak beams.

Puffing with amazement, the man turned to Mr. Lang and said, "I thought the cross would be light. I thought it was hollow. Why do you carry such a heavy cross?"

Mr. Lang drew himself up to his full height and replied with compelling dignity and rebuke: "Sir, if I did not feel the weight of His cross, I could not play His part!"[5]

> *Must Jesus bear the cross alone,*
> *And all the world go free?*
> *No, there's a cross for ev'ryone,*
> *And there's a cross for me.*
>
> *The consecrated cross I'll bear*
> *Till death shall set me free;*
> *And then go home my crown to wear,*
> *For there's a crown for me.*
>   —Thomas Shepherd and others

Jesus calls again in our day, "If anyone would come after me, he must deny himself and take up his cross and follow me" (Matt. 16:24).

8

THE NECESSITY OF
THE CROSS

MATTHEW 27:33-43
CF. MARK 15:22-32; LUKE 23:34-38

They came to a place called Golgotha (which means The Place of the Skull). There they offered Jesus wine to drink, mixed with gall; but after tasting it, he refused to drink it. When they had crucified him, they divided up his clothes by casting lots. And sitting down, they kept watch over him there. Above his head they placed the written charge against him: THIS IS JESUS, THE KING OF THE JEWS. Two robbers were crucified with him, one on his right and one on his left. Those who passed by hurled insults at him, shaking their heads and saying, "You who are going to destroy the temple and build it in three days, save yourself! Come down from the cross, if you are the Son of God!"

In the same way the chief priests, the teachers of the law and the elders mocked him. "He saved others," they said, "but he can't save himself! He's the King of Israel! Let him come down now from the cross, and we will believe in him. He trusts in God. Let God rescue him now if he wants him, for he said, 'I am the Son of God'" *(Matt. 27:33-43)*.

Golgotha, known also as Calvary, exhibits the value God puts on each person.

A tall, lanky backwoodsman from "upriver" country had floated down the Mississippi River aboard a barge loaded with produce for the markets of New Orleans. Taking in sights along the docks, he suddenly came upon a crowd listening to the raucous voice of an auctioneer. Curiosity beckoned until, to his horror, he witnessed a slave auction in progress. He watched as a man was sold and separated from his wife. Children were being taken from the arms of parents and sold to the highest bidders.

Deeply stirred, he lifted a long, muscular arm toward heaven and made a vow: "God helping me, someday I'll strike a death blow to that traffic in human lives."

God heard that vow. And Abraham Lincoln was given opportunity to make it happen. Though Lincoln fulfilled his vow for freedom, it cost him his life.

On Calvary's cross, Jesus was fulfilling a vow He had made before the foundation of the world to strike a death blow to the power of sin. God the Father guided His Son, Jesus, to see that vow brought to completion. Jesus fulfilled His vow to "seek and to save what was lost" (Luke 19:10), but it cost Him His life in a horrible execution.

After Roman soldiers teased and tortured their hapless victim, they mocked Him: "Hail, king of the Jews!" (Mark 15:18). Some of the little men in the streets, grown fearless now that they were lost in the anonymous crowd, reached out and struck Jesus as He passed by. Some sadistic spectators leaned forward and spit in His face.

After He was at last nailed onto the Cross, passersby nonchalantly looked, laughed, and left—"loafers running about in the marketplace of the Spirit."[1]

Jewish leaders stood in full view, shaking with scornful laughter. Poking each other in mock disdain, they shouted, "He saved others . . . but he can't save himself!" (Matt. 27:42).

The Sanhedrin looked with suspicion on all "messiahs," for many self-styled "messiahs" had come and gone.

To them, Jesus was only one more. They argued, "We have heard from the Law that the Christ will remain forever" (John 12:34). Here was final proof that Jesus was not the Messiah: He was about to die! With sneering lips, they shouted, "He saved others . . . but he can't save himself!"

They took note of the Cross without knowing the Savior. These oracles of wisdom volunteered the information: "He saved others . . . but he can't save himself!" Those men didn't know how to interpret Jesus. So familiar with bloody sacrifices and smoking altars, they missed the whole significance of their work in the Temple. Surprisingly, they spoke the truth better than they knew! Their intended insult was actually a great spiritual truth: "He saved others . . . but he can't save himself!"

CHRIST DID SAVE OTHERS

Jesus' whole life confirmed the truth: "He saved others!" Jesus saved others from disability and disease. Even His enemies couldn't deny His power to save. How could they deny the fact that blind Bartimaeus had been given sight and walked before their own eyes? In front of multitudes, Jesus had said to the sick woman: "Daughter, your faith has healed you. Go in peace" (Luke 8:48). How could these priests deny Jesus' power over disease when 10 lepers whom Jesus had cleansed came to the priests themselves for the examination required by Mosaic law? Before many witnesses, Jesus said to the bedfast man suffering from palsy, "Get up, take your mat and go home" (Matt. 9:6).

Jesus saved others from death. The amazing event of Lazarus walking out of the tomb after being dead for more than three days was still fresh in their memories. It was a prelude to God's promise for resurrection life through Jesus Christ. It was only the down payment for greater things yet to come. How could Jesus' enemies deny His raising Lazarus from the dead when so many people had witnessed the event? Lazarus was once again mingling with people in Bethany, a suburb of Jerusalem.

Jesus saved others from sin. The statement "He saved others" extends beyond the physical realm. If the idea that Jesus *saves* is a new thought in your vocabulary, note that this same word means "salvage." Jesus can salvage broken lives, homes gone awry, minds laden with guilt and self-condemnation, even from habits that imprison the will. Jesus is in the business of salvaging those who turn to Him for help.

Jesus saves others for wholeness. He has come to bring completeness and purity within. Religion, reformations, and resolutions are self-induced labors to clean up the outside of the life. But Jesus can cleanse the inside. He came to make men whole—not frustrated contradictions between good and bad impulses clamoring for expression. Many times Jesus said, "Take heart, son; your sins are forgiven" (Matt. 9:2). The author of Hebrews testified: "Therefore he is able to save completely those who come to God through him, because he always lives to intercede for them" (7:25).

In a vision, Martin Luther saw Satan approaching with a large book under his arm. "This book contains the record of the sins of your life," he told Luther.

As Satan began to read, Luther shouted: "Stop! Here is another Book—the Word of God. It says, 'the blood of Jesus his Son purifies us from every sin.'"

Jesus did come to save others!

CHRIST COULD HAVE SAVED HIMSELF

Before His arrest and conviction, Jesus had told His disciples: "I lay down my life—only to take it up again. No one takes it from me, but I lay it down of my own accord" (John 10:17-18). His death was no suicide or martyrdom. His death was so meaningful that He chose to accept it. On the eve of His crucifixion, Jesus prayed: "I have brought you glory on earth by completing the work you gave me to do" (17:4).

Jesus could have saved himself. In fact, as you read the four Gospels, it is startling how often Jesus could have avoided the Cross. But Jesus turned away from easy and popular leadership even though He could have been delivered from the reach of His enemies. Consistently He refused to exercise miraculous powers to win people to himself.

In His last hours, Jesus could have saved himself from the faltering Temple guards. He stopped Peter's futile sword-swinging and said, "Do you think I cannot call on my Father, and he will at once put at my disposal more than twelve legions of angels?" (Matt. 26:53). At His request, angelic hosts and their chariots of fire who had guarded Elisha and his frightened servant would have instantly responded in full battle regalia.

> *They bound the hands of Jesus*
> *in the garden where He prayed.*
> *They led Him through the streets in shame.*
> *They spat upon the Savior,*
> *so pure and free from sin;*
> *They said, "Crucify Him! He's to blame."*
>
> *To the howling mob He yielded;*
> *He did not for mercy cry.*
> *The Cross of shame He took alone.*
> *And when He cried, "It's finished,"*
> *He gave himself to die.*
> *Salvation's wondrous plan was done.*
>
> *He could have called ten thousand angels*
> *To destroy the world and set Him free.*
> *He could have called ten thousand angels,*
> *But He died alone for you and me.* *
> —Ray Overholt

William Booth, founder of the Salvation Army, declared, "It is because Jesus did not come down from the Cross that we believe in Him."[2] He could have saved himself—but if He had, He could not have saved anyone else!

CHRIST WOULD NOT SAVE HIMSELF

Because He loves us, Jesus did not save himself. He chose to save others and deny himself. It was His love, not the nails, that held Him on that Cross!

The Cross was necessary because "without the shedding of blood there is no forgiveness" (Heb. 9:22). At the Lord's last Passover feast on the night before His crucifixion, Jesus symbolized the cup of wine: "This is my blood of the covenant, which is poured out for many for the forgiveness of sins" (Matt. 26:28). He knew what was going to happen—and He intended not to save himself.

As important as His life might be, as valuable as His teachings, and as inspiring as His actions, Jesus' death was more important. By His death He carried out God's plan of reconciliation. On the Cross "God made him who had no sin to be sin for us, so that in him we might become the righteousness of God" (2 Cor. 5:21). Jesus' death was His greatest act of mercy!

One preacher said, "This is why the Gospels devote so much space to His passion and death . . . One third of Matthew, Mark, Luke, and John describe the last week of the Savior's life, His death, and His resurrection. Does not the emphasis tell us how important this death is for us? Read the Epistles of Paul, Peter, and the rest and note how little is said of our Lord's life, but how much is said of His death and resurrection."[3]

Since Jesus would not save himself, religious leaders mocked: "He's the king of Israel! Let him come down now from the cross, and we will believe in him" (Matt. 27:42). Those men had put a price tag on their allegiance—a crossless religion. They were demanding that sacrifice be eliminated as the price of their loyalty. But without Jesus' self-sacrificing love, it would be just another cheap, man-made religion.

"He saved others . . . but he can't save himself!" This insult hurled at Jesus carried a wonderful truth: He could not save himself because He did not *choose* to save himself. He was willing to be spent for God's kingdom to salvage lost men and women.

To those cocky little men wagging their heads in derision, Jesus appeared to be a total failure, a magnificent flop. They mistook the darkness before the dawn of success for the dark clouds of failure. What seemed to be a dismal end proved to be the provision for a great new beginning. Bad Friday turned out to be Good Friday! Only one day would separate the world's saddest day from the world's gladdest day!

In all of this we get a glimpse of the broken heart of God. We see God's great act of mercy for our benefit when the truth becomes clear: "He saved others . . . but he can't save himself!"

A man . . . operated a giant drawbridge. One day he took his young son with him in order to show him what . . . he did every day. He led the young lad down into the cavernous workings of the bridge that they might marvel together over its powerful machinery. While down there the man received a phone call that a train, well ahead of schedule, was speeding toward the bridge. There was just enough time for him to race to the top of the tower and flip the switch to lower it into place. Patiently he instructed his son not to budge from his tight position of safety.

The father reached the tower with just enough time to lower the bridge. In the same split second he looked down to find that his son had moved into the jaws of the powerful machinery. He had to decide between the hundreds of lives speeding toward him in the train or the precious life of his only son. In great pain and anguish he flipped the switch. Down came the bridge, grinding the life out of his son. The train rushed by and as it did he could see people sitting there, in the comfort of their dining cars, chatting merrily with one another, totally oblivious to the enormous sacrifice that had just been made for their lives. Beating his fists on the tower window, the man screamed out against the stiff faces streaking past, a people for whom he had made so dear a sacrifice: "Don't you know that I gave my son for you? Don't you know that you are alive now because he yielded up his life? Does anybody care?"[4]

Can we comprehend the cost for our rescue? Do we reverence the heartbreak of God, who offered His own Son for us? And how shall we respond? Does anybody care?

> *When I survey the wondrous cross*
>   *On which the Prince of Glory died,*
> *My richest gain I count but loss,*
>   *And pour contempt on all my pride.*
>
> *Were the whole realm of nature mine,*
>   *That were a present far too small.*
> *Love so amazing, so divine,*
>   *Demands my soul, my life, my all!*
>   —Isaac Watts

9

"REMEMBER ME"

LUKE 23:32-43

Two other men, both criminals, were also led out with him to be executed. When they came to the place called the Skull, there they crucified him, along with the criminals—one on his right, the other on his left. Jesus said, "Father, forgive them, for they do not know what they are doing." And they divided up his clothes by casting lots.

The people stood watching, and the rulers even sneered at him. They said, "He saved others; let him save himself if he is the Christ of God, the Chosen One."

The soldiers also came up and mocked him. They offered him wine vinegar and said, "If you are the king of the Jews, save yourself."

There was a written notice above him, which read: THIS IS THE KING OF THE JEWS.

One of the criminals who hung there hurled insults at him: "Aren't you the Christ? Save yourself and us!"

But the other criminal rebuked him. "Don't you fear God," he said, "since you are under the same sentence? We are punished justly, for we are getting what our deeds deserve. But this man has done nothing wrong."

Then he said, "Jesus, remember me when you come into your kingdom."

Jesus answered him, "I tell you the truth, today you will be with me in paradise" *(Luke 23:32-43)*.

All through His public ministry, Jesus had been identified as a friend of sinners. Now, He was crucified between two thieves—identifying with sinners even in His death. Centuries earlier, Isaiah prophesied: "He . . . was numbered with the transgressors. For he bore the sin of many, and made intercession for the transgressors" (53:12).

Clovis, king of the Franks, listened intently as someone told him for the first time the story of the crucifixion of Jesus. With deep emotion, he cried out, "If I had been there with my Franks, I would have avenged this wrong!"

Only one voice spoke out at the cross in Jesus' defense. Only a dying thief championed the cause of Christ in that dark hour. He was the first defender of Jesus! In that very same day Judas had betrayed Jesus, Peter had denied Him, His disciples had forsaken and fled, but one of Jesus' companions in death called Him "Lord!" That dying thief prayed sincerely, "Lord, remember me when thou comest into thy kingdom" (Luke 23:42, KJV). With great faith he reached out against the tide of opposition and disbelief! When everything by outward appearances seemed lost, one man sensed the kingliness of Christ and felt that Jesus was marching somehow to a throne.

In spite of the crowd's hatred, scorn, and ridicule, Jesus possessed a power that gave no hint of retaliation. Only love could say, "Father, forgive them, for they do not know what they are doing" (Luke 23:34). Jesus' forgiving spirit won the heart of a hardened criminal. The thief believed even when the disciples doubted. His faith reached out to the One who could not and would not save himself!

Here is both a word of hope and a word of warning: "The thief was saved as he was dying. In modern terms, the clock was almost ready to strike 12. In all the Bible there is only a single case of what we may call 'death-bed repentance.' There is one example, lest some should despair; only one, lest some should presume."[1]

Through the centuries many soul winners have rejoiced that such a story exists to tell someone standing at the gates of eternity. What a beautiful demonstration of the truth that, as long as a man can repent, he can be forgiven!

It is amazing, however, that people can pervert God's goodness into evil. Evil and rebellious hearts have used this incident for an argument for continuing in sin. The conversion of the dying thief must never be used as an encouragement to postpone repentance to the 11th hour, a death-bed conversion. While true repentance is never too late, late repentance is often not true.

A self-righteous fellow procrastinated over coming to Jesus. He said to a friend who cared enough to tell him about Jesus, "Don't worry about me. For me it's one world at a time. I'm going to enjoy this life while it lasts. There's enough time. Near life's end, like the dying thief, I'll turn to God."

His friend responded, "When the end comes, I wonder which dying thief you will be like? There were *two* of them, as you recall."

The lateness of the dying thief's repentance is not the remarkable point of the lesson. Keep in mind that it was his first encounter with Jesus. The amazing thing is that he saw so much in this first meeting with Jesus face-to-face. It was pointed out, "He . . . believed that Jesus would have a kingdom, a kingdom after He was dead, a kingdom though He was crucified. He believed that He was winning for himself a kingdom by those nailed hands and pierced feet . . . He believed that Jesus would have a kingdom in which others would share, and therefore, he aspired to have his portion in it."[2]

The thrilling moment came when the dying thief turned to Jesus and pleaded, "Remember me!" That prayer became the pivotal point in his relationship with Jesus. There were three stages in that relationship: first, he was *against* Jesus; then he was *for* Jesus. Finally, he was *with* Jesus.

THE PENITENT THIEF HAD BEEN AGAINST JESUS

Both Matthew and Mark record how the leaders and passersby mocked and ridiculed Jesus. But Matthew noted, "In the same way the robbers who were crucified with him also heaped insults on him" (27:44). Torn by anguish and hatred, both robbers lashed out at their tormentors and joined with them in antagonizing Jesus. Jesus' whole life had been in vivid contrast with self-seeking Pharisees and in contrast with self-gratifying thieves. His guileless demeanor stirred conflict in their sinful hearts.

Along with others, the penitent thief reacted against Jesus—but every defender of the faith was once its enemy, actively or passively. Many people today live lives of quiet opposition to Jesus. Though not actively opposed to Him, they ignore Him—the greatest insult to the Cross! Practical atheists may believe in God, but to them God makes no difference in how they live.

One woman described her husband: "Bob worked hard for his success, and I worked right along with him. When we were first married, we lived in a little apartment over the garage where he had his shop. Now, 16 years later, he owns his own plant with 50 employees. We have a big house, and we don't have to worry about money as we used to. But I wonder if it was worth it. Bob and I seem to have grown apart. We don't have much to talk about. We were happier when he worked downstairs in that garage."

Many people begin to have the same doubts. Frank, a bank vice president, echoed it: "By any measurement I qualify as 'successful,' but do you know what keeps going through my head? It's that phrase: 'Is this all there is?' I've put in 22 years to get where I am, and none of it seems to mean much anymore."

That's the plight of people who have built their lives

without Christ. Even such spiritual indifference is really against Jesus. Poet Robert Frost wrote these lines:

> *I shall be telling this with a sigh*
> *Somewhere ages and ages hence:*
> *Two roads diverged in a wood, and I—*
> *I took the one less traveled by,*
> *And that has made all the difference.*[3]

THE PENITENT THIEF WAS FOR JESUS

The thief cried out in faith: "Jesus, remember me when you come into your kingdom" (Luke 23:42). Perhaps the mocking of the priests gave him the clue—they called Him a king and a messiah. Suddenly it was clear to him that the One by his side on that central cross was none other than the Suffering Servant of Israel. It was a sudden discovery!

A Sunday School teacher held up a portrait of Jesus. She explained to her class that it was not an actual picture, but an artist's conception of Christ. One little girl commented, "But, you've got to admit it sure *looks* like Him!"

If this was not the Messiah on the central cross, it sure did *seem* like it! Ancient descriptions of the Messiah had told of a Suffering Servant, God's Anointed One! And the dying thief was swayed toward Jesus. He who joined others against Jesus was now for Jesus.

Years ago Gilbert West and Lord Lyttleton, two brilliant young men, agreed to expose the "fictions" of the Bible. West was to make a careful study to dispose the resurrection of Jesus once and for all. Lyttleton's assignment was to disparage the conversion of Paul.

At the appointed time, the two met to compare notes. West, on the basis of his study, had become convinced of the resurrection of Jesus. Lyttleton likewise concluded that Paul had been converted just as the Book of Acts described. Both men published their works and became great defenders of the faith they once sought to destroy. Was that not also true of the apostle Paul?

When the thief pleaded, "Remember me," he was now for Jesus! Notice four basic steps in his pilgrimage.

First, he acknowledged his sin. He said aloud, "We are punished justly, for we are getting what our deeds deserve" (Luke 23:41). He had sinned and he admitted it. He was condemned and deserved it. What a clear confession of guilt! Blaming no one else, he agreed with God that he had sinned. That's the first step to anyone's recovery.

Second, he turned from sin. That turning away is called repentance. He rebuked the other thief, a man who had lived as he and who blasphemed against Jesus: "'Don't you fear God,' he said, 'since you are under the same sentence? We are punished justly'" (Luke 23:40-41).

The penitent thief was turning away from sin in the only way he knew at the moment. He renounced his old attitudes and old ways. One scholar wrote: "Repentance is properly tied to the forsaking of sin, with the genuineness of a man's repentance reflected in his break with sin, at least in attitude of mind. The truly repentant sinner loathes his sin."[4]

Third, he believed in Jesus. What amazing faith! His powerful faith reached out across the shame and mockery of that moment and took hold of the crucified Christ as king! He believed he could trust Jesus, for he said, "This man has done nothing wrong" (Luke 23:41). The penitent thief staked everything on Jesus: "Remember me when you come into your kingdom" (v. 42). He was a drowning man clinging to his only hope—Jesus Christ.

A sailor once was rescued from a rock to which he had clung after his boat capsized in a storm. One coast-guardsman asked, "Didn't you shake with fear during those long hours of waiting?"

"Yes," he replied. "I certainly did. But the rock didn't shake!" The hymnwriter exclaimed:

Jesus, Lover of my soul,
Let me to Thy bosom fly,
While the nearer waters roll,
While the tempest still is high!
Hide me, O my Saviour, hide
Till the storm of life be past.
Safe into the haven guide.
O receive my soul at last!

Other refuge have I none;
Hangs my helpless soul on Thee;
Leave, ah, leave me not alone;
Still support and comfort me!
All my trust on Thee is stayed;
All my help from Thee I bring.
Cover my defenseless head
With the shadow of Thy wing.
—Charles Wesley

Fourth, the penitent thief confessed Jesus as Lord. He begged, "Lord, remember me" (Luke 23:42, KJV). He believed Jesus was Lord of a kingdom and that Jesus was going to that kingdom. The Bible teaches, "If you confess with your mouth, 'Jesus is Lord,' and believe in your heart that God raised him from the dead, you will be saved" (Rom. 10:9). The only member of the crucified man's body that was free to move was his tongue—and with it he confessed Jesus as Lord!

THE PENITENT THIEF IS ASSURED HE WILL BE WITH JESUS

"Then he said, 'Jesus, remember me when you come into your kingdom.'

"Jesus answered him, 'I tell you the truth, today you will be with me in paradise'" (Luke 23:42-43).

Out of fear for the future, a young army officer asked the chaplain, "Sir, pray for me when we leave for the front tomorrow."

The chaplain replied, "I am coming with you!" Whatever he would pray or say would now have a much greater impact on that young officer.

When the penitent thief called to Jesus, Jesus gave him the best news yet: "Today you will be with me in paradise." No sooner had he believed than Jesus Christ assured him of His presence forever. It was God's promise of a great tomorrow. In a single moment, the hopeless person can pass from despair with life to the joy of eternal life beginning here and now.

"Today you will be with me in paradise"—that promise of Jesus sheds light on what lies beyond the grave! "Paradise" *(paradeisos)* came from the Persian word for "park" or "garden." "In the ordinary language used by the Jews, of the unseen world, [paradise] signifies the 'Garden of Eden,' or 'Abraham's bosom'; it represented the locality where the souls of the righteous would find a home, after death separated soul and body."[5]

In Eastern lands the idea of paradise commonly described the garden of the king, a beautiful garden with green lawns and sparkling waters, with the palace as the center feature. Jesus' promise to the penitent thief meant that today not only would he be remembered but also, in close companionship, he would enter into the highest joy of the Kingdom. As in the beginning during man's innocence, paradise was that place where Adam enjoyed the presence of his Creator God. So Jesus assured the dying but penitent thief, "Today you will be with me." Where Jesus is, it is heaven to us!

He who was Jesus' last companion on earth would be Jesus' first companion at the gates of paradise! The robber who had had breakfast in prison with the devil would have supper tonight with Jesus in paradise!

A visitor to New York City got off the subway train at Times Square. Confused about which way to go, he asked one of the subway attendants, "Where is so-and-so street?"

With indifference, the man snarled, "Don't ask me anything about 'up there,' Mister. I know all about down here, but I don't know anything up there."

Thank goodness, the dying thief found Jesus who knew all about "up there"! "Today you will be with me in paradise." And if you have believed in Jesus and trusted Him, you are prepared for heaven—whether you came to Him five minutes ago or 50 years ago. Jesus knows where we are going—and He is going with us. He speaks to us, "Let not your heart be troubled: ye believe in God, believe also in me. In my Father's house are many mansions: if it were not so, I would have told you. I go to prepare a place for you. And if I go and prepare a place for you, I will come again, and receive you unto myself; that where I am, there ye may be also" (John 14:1-3, KJV).

For the Christian, death is never a conclusion—only a sign.

In the African country of Kenya, a gravestone marks the burial place of Lord Baden-Powell, founder of the Boy Scouts. The inscription says: "Lord Baden-Powell, Chief Scout of the World. Born February 22, 1856, died January 8, 1941."

Below that inscription is the symbol scouts have used all over the world, blazed on stumps, traced in the dust of a trail, drawn on a rock. It is a circle with a dot in the center. In scout language it means "I have gone home!"

What good news we have in Jesus! The Bible says, "For it is by grace you have been saved, through faith" (Eph. 2:8). Faith in Jesus was the only door open to the dying thief—and he was willing to trust Jesus to save him. We are saved by simple, childlike trust in the Christ of the Cross! Jesus says, "Him that cometh to me I will in no wise cast out" (John 6:37, KJV). If you come to Jesus, He will never turn you away or ignore you. This same Jesus has a

wonderful place prepared for you, as He did for that penitent thief.

> *The dying thief rejoiced to see*
> *That fountain in his day;*
> *And there may I, tho' vile as he,*
> *Wash all my sins away!*
>   —William Cowper

You'll find life is worth living when you find a God
worth loving!

10

UNVEILING GOD'S HEART

MATTHEW 27:50-51
CF. MARK 15:38; LUKE 23:45

The sun stopped shining *(Luke 23:45)*.
And when Jesus had cried out again in a loud voice, he gave up his spirit.
At that moment the curtain of the temple was torn in two from top to bottom. The earth shook and the rocks split *(Matt. 27:50-51)*.

When we get serious about God, our questions change. We quit giving opinions about God and begin caring about God's opinion of us.

All our opinions added together do not alter God's heart of love. But what majesty He reveals of himself through His Word! The more we study the Bible, the more we know about God. Better yet, the more we know Him!

Matthew, Mark, and Luke jotted down in a sentence or two an interesting note on an event occurring between the crucifixion of Jesus and the joy of the Resurrection: "And when Jesus had cried out again in a loud voice, he gave up his spirit. At that moment the curtain of the temple was torn in two from top to bottom" (Matt. 27:50-51). In our hurry to complete the story of Easter, we could miss a beautiful lesson—the unveiling of God's heart!

The Temple veils hung down about 60 feet. The woven fabric with threads of gold and silver contained 72 twisted plaits of 24 threads each. The curtains were as thick as a man's palm. The veil covered an opening 30 feet wide separating the sanctuary from the inner cubical room called the holy of holies or the most holy place.

Behind the huge veil was the room considered to be the dwelling place of God's presence. In the original Temple built by Solomon, the ark of the covenant was kept in the holy of holies. On the ornate lid of the ark was the mercy seat, where the blood of an innocent, unblemished lamb was poured out. The ritual sacrifice was for the atonement of the sins of God's people.

Once a year the high priest, after strict ceremonial cleansing, would enter the holy of holies behind the veil. The glory of God shone uniquely in that darkened room in an unexplainable manner. However, centuries before Jesus Christ came, the ark of the covenant was lost. Enemies of Israel had destroyed it. The glory of God had departed, but high priests continued the rituals—rituals empty of themselves but symbolic of Him who was to come—the Lamb of God who would take away the sin of the world!

Suddenly, at the moment of Jesus' death on the Cross, that great veil was ripped in two! The rending signaled the removal of that separation between God and man. So that no one could explain the incident away, the mammoth veil was torn from top to bottom! It was a divine rending—not man's.

In this unveiling, we learn some beautiful things about God's heart of love.

THE TORN VEIL DEMONSTRATES GOD'S APPROACHABILITY

In people's minds, the veil of the Temple had excluded ordinary men and women from God. Everyone but the high priest was kept outside. Thus, mystery shrouded the heart of God.

However, when Jesus died, that veil was torn in two.

Light flooded through the gloomy darkness. Excluded mankind was now admitted—the whole world was brought inside! "Through the rent veil of Christ's flesh the way was now opened into the very presence of God."[1]

Now, no man can stand between us and God. We do not need to go through any priest or elder. In Christ every person has direct access to the presence of God. The torn veil is God's visible invitation to approach Him. The psalmist sang, "He who dwells in the shelter of the Most High will rest in the shadow of the Almighty" (Ps. 91:1).

The tearing of the veil represented the removal of all barriers and difficulties and discouragements in our approach to God. Divisions between priest and worshiper have been erased: Jesus' church is the priesthood of believers. Divisions between Jew and Gentile, bond and free were torn asunder when Jesus gave His life on the Cross.

The Bible speaks of those who felt excluded, without hope and without God: "But now in Christ Jesus you who once were far away have been brought near through the blood of Christ. For he himself is our peace, who has made the two one and has destroyed the barrier, the dividing wall of hostility, by abolishing in his flesh the law with its commandments and regulations. . . . For through him we both have access to the Father by one Spirit" (Eph. 2:13-15, 18).

Since God opened the way, we can enter into His presence with boldness—not groveling in the dirt, but as children of God. The author of Hebrews exclaimed, "Therefore, brothers, since we have confidence to enter the Most Holy Place by the blood of Jesus, by a new and living way opened for us through the curtain, that is, his body . . . let us draw near to God" (10:19-20, 22).

The approachability of God is at the very heart of the Christian faith.

A little boy heard the news that his father had just been promoted to the rank of brigadier. Everyone was talking about it, but the boy got very quiet. Finally he asked, "Do you think he will mind if I still call him 'Daddy'?"

Paul declared, "For you did not receive a spirit that makes you a slave again to fear, but you received the Spirit of sonship. And by Him we cry, *'Abba*, Father'" (Rom. 8:15).

God has not shut you out. He invites you into His presence, into His forgiveness, into His redeeming work through Jesus Christ: "Let us then approach the throne of grace with confidence, so that we may receive mercy and find grace to help us in our time of need" (Heb. 4:16).

THE TORN VEIL DEMONSTRATES GOD'S AVAILABILITY

In people's minds, God's presence was confined to the holy of holies. Religious expressions and spiritual exercises were directed toward the location of the most holy place. But God never did want to be a "God in a box." He never intended for us to have a secondhand approach to His presence.

When Jesus died, God tore that veil from above to make it known that He wanted out! He did not want us to conceive of Him as located in a certain place, thus unavailable. We can worship God anytime, anywhere, "in spirit and in truth" (John 4:24). God is on call, available when and where we need Him. Wherever we are, God is— and He is willing and ready to communicate with us.

My sin separated me from God—but *I* moved, not Him. Sin brings spiritual separation. Sin is the great divider between God and man. That empty gulf between God and me left me incomplete. In my frustrations, I tried many ways to improve—but nothing worked. I could not bridge the gap between God and me. There was nothing I could do.

Then I realized that it had already been done—by Jesus at the Cross. He is God's great provision for my spiritual need. Jesus bridged the gap of separation. All I had to do was trust His completed work! He is always there when I need Him.

We can find God everywhere and miss Him anywhere. Sin is the great hindrance. Sin is the barrier. However, the good news is that when God tore the veil, He did not rip a little piece of the corner. God rent it right down the middle—60 feet high! He didn't just tear a little bit so that we could peek in. He ripped it from top to bottom—an entrance big enough for the greatest of sinners.

If it had been only a tiny hole, maybe a few lesser offenders could creep through to God's grace and glory. But God performed an act of abounding mercy: the veil was rent right down the middle so that even the chief of sinners is made available to God's love and compassion.

God is available to help you and me. Living in His holy presence enables us to live a life of holiness. He is our Eternal Contemporary.

A pastor said to his church custodian, "I am concerned about an old, shabby man who goes into the church every day at noon. I've watched him through the parsonage window. He stays only a few minutes, but it seems rather strange. Since we have those expensive altar furnishings, I wish you'd keep an eye open. If you get a chance, question the old fellow."

For many days the custodian watched. Every day at noon the old man came and then left quickly. Finally he asked the stranger, "Sir, why do you go into the church every day?"

"I go to pray," the old man replied quietly.

The custodian said, "But, friend, you don't stay long enough to pray. I've watched you. You just go up to the altar every day and then come away. You're there only a few moments."

The old man smiled. "Yes, that's true. I cannot pray a

long prayer. Every day at noon I just come in and say, 'Jesus, it's Jim checking in.' Then I wait a minute and come out. It's just a little prayer, but I guess He hears me."

Months passed, and one day old Jim was hit by a truck. He was taken to the city hospital to be cared for while his broken leg mended.

The ward where Jim stayed had been a tough spot for the nurses. The men all grumbled and complained. However, slowly things changed. The men began taking their medicine without arguing, eating their food without complaint, and settling down at night without disturbance.

One day a nurse actually heard laughter coming from that ward. She exclaimed, "What's happened to you all? Your attitudes are so different!"

A patient replied, "It's old Jim. He's always so happy; he never complains, even though he's in pain."

She looked at old Jim's silver hair and peaceful, quiet eyes: "Well, Jim, the men say you're responsible for the change in this ward. They say you're always happy."

"Yes, Nurse. I'm happy. I can't help it. You see, Nurse, it's my Visitor. Every day He makes me happy."

The nurse was puzzled. She had noticed that Jim's chair was always empty on visiting days. He had no relatives. "Your visitor?" she asked. "But when does he come?"

"Every day," Jim replied, his eyes growing brighter.

"Yes, every day at noon He comes and stands by my bed. When I see Him, He smiles and says, 'Jim, it's Jesus checking in!'"

The Bible says, "I sought the LORD, and he answered me; he delivered me from all my fears. Those who look to him are radiant; their faces are never covered with shame. This poor man called, and the LORD heard him; he saved him out of all his troubles. The angel of the LORD encamps around those who fear him, and he delivers them. Taste and see that the LORD is good; blessed is the man who takes refuge in him" (Ps. 34:4-8).

THE TORN VEIL DEMONSTRATES GOD'S AFFECTION

Mark's Gospel contains little of Jesus' teachings and discourses. This account of Jesus' life and ministry is simple, lacking the symbolic interests so often developed by the other Gospel writers. Thus, Mark records the rending of the veil in a simple, straightforward, matter-of-fact narrative.

The Gospel of Mark begins with the statement: "The beginning of the gospel about Jesus Christ, the Son of God" (1:1). All through his Gospel, Mark underlines the divine Sonship of Jesus. At Jesus' baptism, God announced that Jesus is His Son: "You are my Son, whom I love; with you I am well pleased" (v. 11). At Jesus' transfiguration, God reassured, "This is my Son, whom I love. Listen to him!" (9:7). At Jesus' crucifixion, God responded as would a Jewish father at the death of his son.

For example, what did Jacob do when he saw the multicolored coat of his beloved Joseph drenched in blood, convinced that his son was dead? Jacob rent his garment as an expression of deepest sorrow. He reached up and ripped his clothes from the top, baring his brokenhearted chest. What did Job do when he got the shocking news of the death of his children? Job rent his clothes as an expression of deepest sorrow.

When Jesus bowed His head and died, God rent the veil from top to bottom, symbolically exposing His heart of sorrow—His suffering love.

By that vivid gesture, God indicated to Jesus' followers that He had personally been close by during the whole, terrible ordeal. God is not distant and unfeeling. He did not coldly send His Son to a cross. God has mourned the tragedy of sin from the start. He loves you and me so much that He willingly allowed His own grieving heart to be broken. "For God so loved the world, that he gave his only begotten Son, that whosoever believeth in him should not perish, but have everlasting life" (John 3:16, KJV).

You can trust God with your inner self. You can trust Him to bring healing to your broken heart. You can trust Him to reach across the great gulf of your sins and bridge the broken fellowship through the Cross. You can talk to Him, confess every sin, every failure, every frustration.

That torn veil tells us that He is approachable, He is available, and He is deeply concerned for you. Goethe said, "If I were God, this world of sin and suffering would break my heart." When Jesus died, bearing our sins, it *did* break God's heart, but He knew it was worth it! The Bible says, "This is how God showed his love among us: He sent his one and only Son into the world that we might live through him. This is love: not that we loved God, but that he loved us and sent his Son as an atoning sacrifice for our sins" (1 John 4:9-10).

11

THE EULOGY OF JESUS

MARK 15:37-39
CF. MATTHEW 27:54; LUKE 23:47

> With a loud cry, Jesus breathed his last.
> The curtain of the temple was torn in two from top to bottom. And when the centurion, who stood there in front of Jesus, heard his cry and saw how he died, he said, "Surely this man was the Son of God!" *(Mark 15:37-39)*

About midday of that dark Friday outside Jerusalem, Jesus uttered His boyhood prayer: "Father, into your hands I commit my spirit" (Luke 23:46). Then Jesus bowed His head gently—and died.

At that moment, the ornate, sacred veil of the Temple, blocking the entrance into the most holy place, was torn from top to bottom. Additionally, "the sun stopped shining" (Luke 23:45)—literally, "The sun failed." "The Greek word *fail* is the equivalent of our English word *eclipse;* but it could not have been a natural eclipse, because at Passover time the moon was practically full and on the opposite side of the earth from the sun. So this was an unnatural darkness, a mystery mentioned by Matthew,

Mark, and Luke with no attempt at explanation."[1] The earth convulsed. Rocks cracked. Strange phenomena took place. "And when the centurion, who stood there in front of Jesus, heard his cry and saw how he died, he said, 'Surely this man was the Son of God!'" (Mark 15:39).

These are the only recorded words spoken over the body of Jesus. The Holy Spirit seems to have appointed the Roman centurion to give the appropriate eulogy to the life of Jesus. Without hesitation or apology, he exclaimed, "Surely this man was the Son of God!" What more could be said?

The eulogy of Jesus was spoken not by religious leaders nor a faithful follower, but by a hardened, pagan Roman soldier who had ordered the nails driven into the hands and feet of Jesus.

While history is obscure concerning him, tradition claims this centurion was named Longinus, "who was led by the miracles which accompanied the death of Christ, to acknowledge Him to be the Son of God, and to be a herald of His resurrection, and was ultimately himself put to death for the sake of Christ in Cappadocia. St. Chrysostom repeats the common report, that on account of his faith he was at last crowned with martyrdom."[2]

By watching the scene of Jesus' crucifixion this good man was changed. It was a remarkable conversion—right at the Cross! But Jesus' death did what His life could not do—it broke the hard hearts of men. Earlier, Jesus had said, "But I, when I am lifted up from the earth, will draw all men to myself" (John 12:32). Already the magnet of the Cross had begun its work! Ever since, the repetition of the story of the Cross has a strange power to change people's minds and hearts. Sometimes they who hear it for the first time are drawn by the Holy Spirit.

The eulogy of Jesus has a life-giving power in it! What was wrapped up in those simple words, "Surely this man was the Son of God"?

THE CENTURION RESPONDED TO THE GOODNESS OF JESUS

In Luke's Gospel, the Roman centurion Longinus is recorded as saying, "Surely this was a righteous man" (Luke 23:47). The Greek work for righteous, *dikaios*, describes being right, or right conduct judged by divine standards and human standards. That's how the Roman centurion saw Jesus. He had watched the drama unfold between Jesus and His tormentors.

First, Longinus saw the goodness of Jesus in His reactions. There had been no retaliation—just a prayer: "Father, forgive them, for they do not know what they are doing" (Luke 23:34). Concern for others loomed large, even when it seemed all was lost. The goodness of a man's character is seen in the crucible of tragedy and sorrow and persecution. That quality of righteousness was evidenced in Jesus.

Second, Longinus saw Jesus in contrast with the world's values. James S. Stewart wrote:

> The death of Jesus has *revealed sin in its true nature.* Let us remember that the evil things which put Jesus on the cross were by no means unfamiliar or abnormal. Self-interest in Caiaphas, fear in Pilate, impurity in Herod, anger and spite in the crowd—these were the things which, coming in contact with the sinless One, deliberately compassed His death. . . .

> Jesus was crucified by the ordinary sins of every day. We are all in this together. Our heart and conscience tell us, when we stand on Calvary, that what we see there is our own work, and that the sins we so lightly condone result always in the crucifixion of the Son of God.[3]

Third, Longinus saw Jesus' innocence. "Beyond all doubt . . . this man was innocent" (Luke 23:47, NEB). Recognizing the purity of Jesus' human nature, he saw Christ as faultless, guiltless, innocent. Bad deeds spring from bad nature—and the centurion viewed Jesus at the Cross as good and just.

THE CENTURION RESPONDED TO THE GODLIKENESS OF JESUS

Both Matthew and Mark recorded the centurion's declaration: "Surely this man was the Son of God!" However, the Greek text has no definite article. It says, "This man was Son of God!" Commonly, in Jesus' day and in Bible-times cultures, the idea "son of" was employed to describe a particular characteristic.

Barnabas, son of consolation, designated that Barnabas was characterized by his gift of counseling. James and John, known as "sons of thunder," were noisy, competitive, and unpredictable. And the Roman centurion had observed godlikeness in Jesus! "Son of God" can convey the idea of one who possesses the godlike qualities of love and forgiveness, righteousness and holiness.

At the Cross, Longinus noticed that Jesus' love was reaching out to all. Amid His sufferings, Jesus forgave sins as God would—not as men would: "Father, forgive them . . . Today you will be with me in paradise" (Luke 23:34, 43). Men love their friends and hate their enemies—but Jesus loved and forgave His enemies.

In the secret room of the Last Supper, Philip had said to Jesus, "Lord, show us the Father and that will be enough for us" (John 14:8).

Jesus' response staggered them that night: "Anyone who has seen me has seen the Father" (John 14:9).

At the Cross, God's almighty love is revealed through Jesus. Jesus did not die to appease an angry God nor to try to persuade God to change His mind toward us. God never has to be persuaded to love us! As James S. Stewart put it, "Calvary was not an inducement Jesus offered to God; it was God's own love in action . . . The cross reveals the heart of the eternal. It makes grace real. It makes love available for needy souls. It reconciles the sinful and brings the world to God's feet."[4]

A small boy stood with his older brother, looking at a large portrait of their father who had died when the boy was only a baby. The youngest asked, "Henry, what was Father like?"

The older brother tried to describe their father. He had been a good man, strong, kind, honest, and handsome. However, the small boy had difficulty visualizing his father's characteristics. At last he interrupted his older brother: "Tell me one thing, Henry. Was Father anything like you?"

"Well," the boy admitted, "friends of our family who knew him best say I am the living image of Dad."

With his heart aglow and a smile lighting his face, the lad walked away saying, "Now I know exactly what my dad was like. He was just like my brother Henry!"

Jesus was God made visible to our world. In Him we see the Father, for they are exactly alike! "Surely this man was the Son of God!"

THE CENTURION RESPONDED TO THE GRANDEUR OF JESUS

Matthew's Gospel says: "At that moment the curtain of the temple was torn in two from top to bottom. The earth shook and the rocks split. The tombs broke open and the bodies of many holy people who had died were raised to life. . . . When the centurion and those with him who were guarding Jesus saw the earthquake and all that had happened, they were terrified, and exclaimed, 'Surely he was the Son of God!'" (27:51-52, 54).

The unusual phenomenon surrounding Jesus' life and death seemed to climax at the Cross! It was as though nature itself was bearing witness to the fact that Christ was more than man—He was the Son of God! He reveals the glory of God. As Paul wrote, "He is the image of the invisible

God, the firstborn over all creation. For by him all things were created: things in heaven and on earth, visible and invisible, whether thrones or powers or rulers or authorities; all things were created by him and for him" (Col. 1:15-16).

The eulogy of Jesus by the Roman centurion comes like a doxology. He praised God and kept on glorifying God for what he had seen and heard. There's reason to glory—as Cyprian said, "The Son of God suffered to make us sons of God!"[5]

Trying to take it all in, the centurion exclaimed, "Surely this man was the Son of God!"

One preacher remarked,

> The centurion said what he said to glorify God . . . A song was born in the heart of this army officer as he looked upon the scene and weighed the evidence. The cross was the place for a doxology. Someone should have sung the praises of God's grace on that occasion. But the temple choirs could not sing His praise at Calvary. They were out of tune! Nor could the priests, accustomed to chanting many of the old psalms of praise. There was no song of joy in their hearts. Even the disciples were so filled with fear and misunderstanding that they could not sing. But God must have a song. And an army officer . . . gave the doxology . . . The word from Luke, which is translated "glorified," is from the same root as our word "doxology."[6]

The voice that commanded the nails to be driven through the hands of Jesus now praises God!

Jesus had asked earlier, "What think ye of Christ? whose son is he?" (Matt. 22:42, KJV). That's the question facing each of us today. If we open our hearts to the Holy Spirit, we can see the goodness of Jesus, the godlikeness of Jesus, and the grandeur of Jesus! "For God, who said, 'Let light shine out of darkness,' made his light shine in our hearts to give us the light of the knowledge of the glory of God in the face of Christ" (2 Cor. 4:6). We must yield our lives to the Christ of Calvary. Our eternal destiny hangs upon the answer we give.

During her coronation week, Queen Victoria of England sat in the royal box during the performance of Handel's *Messiah*. The lady-in-waiting explained to the new, young queen, "When they begin the 'Hallelujah Chorus,' everyone will rise and remain standing until the music stops. However, it is royal etiquette that the Queen should remain seated."

The orchestra played that majestic music and the great choir unfolded the grandeur of the text. When they reached the "Hallelujah Chorus," the people stood with bowed heads. The queen was deeply moved, her eyes filled with tears, her heart melted by the grace and glory of God.

When the chorale and symphony came to that burst of melody, "King of kings and Lord of lords," in spite of royal etiquette, the young queen stood to her feet with bowed head.

Years later, the chaplain to the queen visited her when she was ill. Having read a book on the second coming of Jesus, she asked the chaplain, "What do you think about the second coming of the Lord?"

He said, "Your Majesty, why have you asked me that question?"

"Oh," she said, "I wish He would come while I am alive, for nothing would give me more pleasure than, with my own hands, to place at His feet the crown of the British Empire!"

As a young woman, she had crowned Jesus King of Kings and Lord of Lords. Now, in her old age, she was willing to give Christ every crown God had given her.

I pray that the goodness, godlikeness, and grandeur of God's Son, Jesus, will persuade you to give Him your soul, your life, your all!

Dr. Glenn Clark, once a president of the Christian Endeavor youth organization, held up a piece of yellow paper before a convention of 20,000 young people following

World War II. "I have a telegram from Japan," he announced.

Silence fell on all as they strained to listen. The telegram contained only three little words: "Make Jesus King!"

That's the urgency of this sacred moment: "Make Jesus King!"

An actor struggled with the role of the Roman centurion in the 1975 film *Jesus of Nazareth*. Finally he stared intently at the cross and let Jesus' utterances from the Cross burn into his thoughts. Suddenly he had a vision of Christ—"pain-seared, sweat-stained, with blood flowing down from thorns pressed deep." The actor had a profound spiritual experience that touched his life. He concluded, "As that centurion learned 2,000 years ago, I too have found that you simply cannot come close to Jesus without being changed."[7]

Do you know Jesus—Jesus, the Son of God? He invites you to come to Him. You cannot come close to Jesus without being changed!

12

THE BURIAL OF JESUS

MATTHEW 27:57-60
CF. MARK 15:42-46; LUKE 23:50-54; JOHN 19:38-42

As evening approached, there came a rich man from Arimathea, named Joseph *(Matt. 27:57)*.

Now Joseph was a disciple of Jesus, but secretly because he feared the Jews *(John 19:38)*.

. . . a member of the Council, a good and upright man, who had not consented to their decision and action *(Luke 23:50-51)*.

Going to Pilate, he asked for Jesus' body, and Pilate ordered that it be given to him *(Matt. 27:58)*.

With Pilate's permission, he came and took the body away. He was accompanied by Nicodemus, the man who earlier had visited Jesus at night *(John 19:38-39)*.

Joseph took the body, wrapped it in a clean linen cloth, and placed it in his own new tomb that he had cut out of the rock. He rolled a big stone in front of the entrance to the tomb and went away *(Matt. 27:59-60)*.

In San José, Costa Rica, my wife and I entered an old Catholic church. We slipped down the side aisles, viewing dramatic portrayals of the Passion Week of Jesus' last days before His burial. Of course, there stood a crucifix with its vivid color and intense countenance. I had seen crucifixes before—and always preferred the empty crosses of the Protestant tradition. However, in the back corner of the large sanctuary was a glass case. As I approached it, I saw the form of a man lying down encased in glass.

I had seen mummified dead before. In the dim light, I realized that this still form was a life-size portrayal of Jesus wrapped in graveclothes. Never in my life had I seen an image of Jesus lying in state. Something about that—something unexplainable—repulsed me. It seemed out of place in a church! Yet it did bring home to me the reality of Jesus, dead and buried, as nothing else had ever done to me.

Yes, it was repulsive! The thought of my Jesus—dead, lifeless, and unresponsive—*is* repulsive. If that's where the story had ended, my hopes would have been dashed to pieces, my dreams broken at my feet, my deep need to be reconciled with God unfulfilled. Jesus in a grave!

How else could Joseph of Arimathea have felt as night came that dark, dismal Friday? Seeing what he had seen, knowing no more than he could have known, it took courage and love to step out of the shadows and personally handle the limp, broken body of Jesus—bloodied, torn, cold!

All four Gospel writers include this act of pity and devotion by the heretofore unknown Jew, Joseph of Arimathea. The Gospel accounts tell us that he was a councillor, a good man, rich and righteous, watching and waiting for the coming of the kingdom of God. But Joseph was also a secret disciple of Jesus. He had not consented to the actions taken by the Sanhedrin to crucify Jesus—but he feared what the Jews might think if they found out that he was a follower of Jesus.

We don't know whether Joseph had been present during the deliberations. But he didn't come out strongly and say, "I am for Jesus!" Fear kept him in secrecy. The high ideals of men are often betrayed by the fear of peer pressure. Real statesmen enunciate the great principles of truth and justice regardless of the cost. Politicians betray principles to maintain the ideals of the majority of voters—right or wrong. The Bible says, "Fear of man will prove to be a snare" (Prov. 29:25). Fear had kept Joseph silent when he should have been forceful.

Being wealthy, Joseph might have been too cautious. Maybe he was hesitant too long because he had more to lose than most. Since he held high office, Joseph moved in influential circles—but he remained silent when Jesus needed him!

The spectacular, the dramatic, and the gruesome are over now. The curious crowd has melted away. Shopkeepers have returned to their booths. The rocky hilltop is almost vacated now. The horrors of crucifixion have faded. The dull pain of memory mingles with the respect one gives to the body of a friend.

Suddenly, Joseph of Arimathea moves out of his secrecy and claims the body of Jesus—at all costs. Joseph's final courtesy reveals something about his relationship to Jesus.

JOSEPH REVEALS AN ANNOUNCEMENT OF DISCIPLESHIP

While Jesus had been executed under Roman law, Jewish law declared that a criminal could not be left hanging dead all night—especially when the next day was the Sabbath. Mosaic law said, "If a man guilty of a capital offense is put to death and his body is hung on a tree, you must not leave his body on the tree overnight. Be sure to bury him that same day" (Deut. 21:22-23).

Since no one usually claimed the bodies of criminals, they were normally taken down and left on the ground for vultures, wild dogs, and vermin to share. Mount Calvary had been named "Golgotha," meaning "The Place of the Skull," probably because it was littered with skulls left from previous crucifixions.

Joseph acted immediately. Going to the governor, Pontius Pilate, he said: "I want the body of Jesus. I am His friend. I am His disciple. I've been slow to admit it publicly and openly, but I am His follower. Please, let me take His body and bury it. I have a new tomb. It's never been used before. Let me bury Jesus in my family's tomb—the best that money can buy!"

Pilate gave permission for Jesus' corpse to be taken down and allowed Joseph custody. In that action, an ancient prophecy was fulfilled: "He was assigned a grave . . . with the rich in his death" (Isa. 53:9).

Again, the death of Jesus did what His life could not do! Joseph was drawn from secrecy into the open by the death of Jesus. Nothing can move men's hearts like the sight of the crucified Christ. William Barclay put it well:

> Joseph was another of these people for whom the Cross of Jesus did what not even the life of Jesus could do. When he had seen Jesus alive he had felt His attraction, but had gone no further. But when he saw Jesus die—and he must have been present at the crucifixion—his heart was broken in love. First the centurion, then Joseph—it is an amazing thing how soon Jesus' words came true that when He was lifted up from the earth He would draw all men unto Him (John 12:32).[1]

Along the coastline float buoys with bells swinging on them. These bells warn of shoals, rocks, and reefs. When the sky is clear and the weather is light, the bell is somewhat quiet. But when storms come, the winds blow, and the waves rush in, those bells clang their sonorous warning for seamen to hear.

Joseph was one of those good men who remains silent when everything is calm. But when the storms come, they will be forced to speak out—and will do it clearly!

When Joseph publicly declared himself a disciple of Jesus, he did so at great personal risk. He could well lose everything—including his life. However, he did not hesitate to admit he was a follower of Jesus in this great crisis.

George W. Truett told of a presidential candidate many years ago. One Sunday, during the campaign, the candidate went to church in Cincinnati. The pastor spoke that day with anointing. The invitation to meet Christ was given: "If there are men here who want to be saved, I wish they would come and kneel down at this front pew, and we will pray for them."

The presidential candidate was stricken in his soul and started up front. His group of political advisers tried to stop him by warning, "You can't afford to do that! You're a candidate for the presidency of this country!"

The man turned to them and replied, "I am a candidate for heaven. I can afford it and I am going. I am a sinner, and I know it. My life is being wasted, and I know it. I am missing the true mark, and I know it. I am neglecting God's mercy, and I know it. I want that man to pray for me."

Out he stepped, down to the front of the sanctuary to meet Jesus, leaving his trembling politicians behind.[2]

Don't go on in confusion and darkness. When Jesus calls you, stand up and declare, "I am for Christ! I choose to go with Jesus!" Come out of hiding if you love Jesus!

When Joseph of Arimathea announced his discipleship to Jesus, a most wonderful thing happened. When he came out for Christ, another man from the Sanhedrin stepped forward—an older man, Nicodemus, who had met Jesus alone one night a long time before. Nicodemus, who had been interested in Jesus, followed in Joseph's steps and said, "I want to help bury Him. I am His friend too."

Wouldn't you step out and make known that you, too, are Jesus' friend? Somebody is waiting to follow. Someone is watching for your actions. Someone will be influenced by your decision. Someone will gain courage as you step out for Jesus Christ. William Gladstone said, "One example is worth a thousand arguments." As a songwriter urged,

> *Ye that are men now serve Him,*
> *Against unnumbered foes;*
> *Let courage rise with danger,*
> *And strength to strength oppose.*
> —George Duffield, Jr.

JOSEPH REVEALS AN ACT OF DEVOTION

In that empty hollowness of cleaning up after a party, Joseph of Arimathea begins the loathsome, painful task of preparing the body of his Master for burial. Tenderly, Jesus is lifted down from the Cross, the nails loosed from the crossbar; the blood-caked beard and hair gently combed out; the broken, tortured body washed. Assisted by Nicodemus, fine linen was wrapped around, folded with myrrh and aloes to preserve the body. The quality of a culture can be judged by its respect for the dead. At high personal cost, Joseph did what he could to demonstrate his love and respect for Jesus.

The rock-hewn, sandstone sepulchre, a type cherished by every Israelite, Joseph willingly gave for Jesus. Little did he know it was only a temporary arrangement!

One of my church members wrote these lines, titled "Joseph of Arimathea":

> *A peaceful tomb I had acquired,*
> *A cool and quiet place:*
> *A man of means prepares ahead*
> *A private, ample space.*
>
> *When Jesus Christ was crucified—*
> *This matchless One on whom*
> *I, Joseph, had believed,*
> *I gave to Him my tomb.*
>
> *How could I think a sealed-up grave*
> *Could hold Divinity?*
> *Christ rose to live in hearts of men,*
> *And His Spirit lives in me.*
> —Mabel Cobb

Since criminals were not buried in their fathers' tombs, it was a very special act of devotion when Joseph of Arimathea surrendered his unused tomb for Jesus.

By touching the dead body of Jesus, Joseph willingly brought upon himself ceremonial impurity. For a Jew, it was considered "unclean" to touch a dead body and would render one cut off from religious ceremonies for several days. With the nightfall of Sabbath, especially during Passover time, Joseph would be excluded from the Temple. That judgment of "uncleanness" was deeply significant to religious Jews. Having handled Jesus, Joseph was now considered defiled—unfit to participate in worship.

Sometimes yet today, a person who comes out for Christ is excluded, made an object of scorn, judged, and condemned by the crowd. Some persons are branded by others as fanatics if they would follow Jesus. Paul wrote,

> But whatever was to my profit I now consider loss for the sake of Christ. What is more, I consider everything a loss compared to the surpassing greatness of knowing Christ Jesus my Lord, for whose sake I have lost all things. I consider them rubbish, that I may gain Christ and be found in him, not having a righteousness of my own that comes from the law, but that which is through faith in Christ—the righteousness that comes from God and is by faith. I want to know Christ and the power of his resurrection and the fellowship of sharing in his sufferings, becoming like him in his death, and so, somehow, to attain to the resurrection from the dead *(Phil. 3:7-11).*

JOSEPH REVEALS AN ATTITUDE OF DESPAIR

The pervading gloom of this picture is the fact that Joseph and Nicodemus, these secret disciples of Jesus, handled only a *dead* Christ! Though in an act of devotion, Joseph gave Jesus his tomb when He was dead; he had remained silent when Jesus was alive. One of the great tragedies is that we keep our bouquets and garlands of praise until our friends are dead and gone. How much better it is to share the beauty of love and praise and joy while our loved ones are still alive!

Joseph and Nicodemus, while they believed in Jesus, saw their last opportunity slip away. Though they gave their best in those last moments, their Christ lay dead.

In a South American church hangs a painting of a surgical operating room. It is a contemporary scene with doctors dressed as today. It is a strange picture, for the patient upon the operating table is a crucifix, a dead Jesus. Someone called it "An Autopsy on a Dead Christ."

Many churches act like that. The dynamic of the new life is missing—the life of a risen Christ in His believers, who are made alive in Him. All that remains is a cold, dead formalism. Songs and sermons feel more like an autopsy of what was than a celebration of the life in Christ that now is. The joy is missing! The Spirit of God is quenched! The cold chills of legalism have gripped the throat of a gospel of love and are choking out the song of joy!

But what else can one expect from a stoic, fearful, secret disciple? Where Jesus really is, the secrecy will kill the discipleship, or the discipleship will kill the secrecy! Though Joseph and Nicodemus did what they could, they left the graveyard with heavy hearts and deep despair.

Clarence Macartney related:

> Among the interesting relics of Thomas Jefferson is his copy of the New Testament. He has gone through the Gospels, scoring out with his pen all passages which present Jesus as a supernatural Person. The records of His miraculous birth and all the miracles are deleted, together with all statements which declare Jesus to be the Son of God. In this deleted New Testament, the Gospel of Matthew ends with these words: "And he rolled a great stone to the door of the sepulchre, and departed" (Matt. 27:60).[3]

As far as Joseph could see, that was the conclusion. There seems to be a terrible finality about gravestones. Jesus was dead, but they had not lost their love for Him.

They still believed in Him. But they had lost hope. For them, the last glimmer of light had flickered out.

So they rolled a great stone over the door, and departed.

Men had written "THE END."

God wrote "TO BE CONTINUED"!

13

I SERVE A RISEN SAVIOR

MARK 16:1-8

When the Sabbath was over, Mary Magdalene, Mary
the mother of James, and Salome bought spices so
that they might go to anoint Jesus' body. Very early
on the first day of the week, just after sunrise, they
were on their way to the tomb and they asked each
other, "Who will roll the stone away from the entrance of the tomb?"

But when they looked up, they saw that the
stone, which was very large, had been rolled away.
As they entered the tomb, they saw a young man
dressed in a white robe sitting on the right side, and
they were alarmed.

"Don't be alarmed," he said. "You are looking for
Jesus the Nazarene, who was crucified. He has risen!
He is not here. See the place where they laid him. But
go, tell his disciples and Peter, 'He is going ahead of
you into Galilee. There you will see him, just as he
told you.'"

Trembling and bewildered, the women went out
and fled from the tomb. They said nothing to anyone,
because they were afraid *(Mark 16:1-8)*.

The battle raged between Napoleon's French forces and
the British led by Wellington. England anxiously awaited
word of the outcome.

A sailing ship crossed the English Channel and approached England's southern coast. Observers at Winches-
ter Cathedral watched a sailor on deck pick up his colored

semaphore flags. He began spelling out the long-awaited message: **W-E-L-L-I-N-G-T-O-N D-E-F-E-A-T-E-D.** Suddenly dense fog swirled across the deck, engulfing the ship from sight.

The sad, heart-wrenching news of the incomplete message was sent to London and swept the nation with gloom and despair: "Wellington defeated."

Finally, after long hours of waiting, the thick fog lifted. Again, the man on the deck picked up the semaphore flags and signaled to the cathedral. He then began spelling out the *complete* message of the battle: **W-E-L-L-I-N-G-T-O-N D-E-F-E-A-T-E-D T-H-E E-N-E-M-Y!**

In the wake of the preceding gloomy report of defeat, the good news of victory spread across England like a prairie fire racing the wind. British hearts were lifted with joy: *Wellington defeated the enemy!*

Centuries ago on a Judean hill, Jesus dangled in death on an executioner's cross. That dark, gloomy day dashed the hopes of the world. Jesus died!

Jesus' disciples despaired at that incomplete message: **"Jesus defeated!"** With shattered hopes, broken dreams, and empty-handed faith, followers of Jesus despairingly cried, "But we had hoped that he was the one who was going to redeem Israel" (Luke 24:21).

Shrouded in a fog of despondency, three ladies walked to Jesus' tomb on the following Sunday morning. Out of respect, they intended to anoint Jesus' body and finish proper burial preparations.

To their surprise, morning mists had lifted—and, lo, the angel of the Lord stood at the empty tomb. He signaled the *complete* message: **"Jesus defeated death!"**

The Easter angel told them four important things.

"FEAR NOT!"

"Don't be alarmed" (Mark 16:6). The angel urged in effect: "Don't be afraid of those things you don't understand.

Don't be amazed! Don't cast aside your confidence in Jesus because you can't comprehend what has happened!"

What a tremendous mystery the Resurrection is—to those three ladies and to us today! But the empty tomb gives reason to break the paralyzing grip of fear. Because Jesus lives, we, too, shall live! A hopeless end has been replaced with endless hope.

On a Good Friday during World War II, a young American soldier was severely wounded in battle. Though he called for help, no one came. He tried to signal airplanes buzzing overhead—but no response. Finally he slipped into unconsciousness.

A medical team rescued him. On Easter Sunday he regained consciousness and found himself in a field hospital. The chaplain stood beside him. As they conversed, the soldier said, "Chaplain, you can stand anything on Good Friday when you're certain of Easter morning!"

Easter's resurrection signals the beginning of great joy. Jesus defeated death! In our age of doubt and worry, the angel reminds us: "Fear not" (Matt. 28:5, KJV). Keep a simple, childlike trust in our risen Lord.

A pastor stood outside looking into a department store window at a painting that portrayed Jesus on the Cross. A little boy came and stood looking also. The minister asked him, "Do you know who He is?"

The lad frowned: "That's Jesus. Those are soldiers standing around. That woman crying is His mother."

The pastor nodded and walked on. But the boy pursued him: "Mister, I wasn't finished. Jesus rose again!" The lad grinned and ran away, happy to tell such good news.

I especially like the completeness of Jesus' victory over death: "There was a violent earthquake, for an angel of the Lord came down from heaven and, going to the tomb, rolled back the stone *and sat on it*" (Matt. 28:2, emphasis added). Ancient kings often sat on the backs of conquered kings or used them for footstools. It was a sign of complete victory. The angel of the Lord removed the stone at the tomb and sat on it! Not only was death defeated, but the Lord added insult to injury! Death was totally conquered. The angel shows us complete victory over the power of death. The grim, sinister powers of evil were raided by the power of Jesus Christ. *Fear not! Jesus defeated death!*

"LOOK ELSEWHERE!"

The angel said, "You are looking for Jesus the Nazarene, who was crucified. He has risen! He is not here. See the place where they laid him" (Mark 16:6). I told my wife, Ruth, that I'd like to have inscribed on my tombstone— "He isn't here yet!"

At Jesus' empty tomb, the epitaph is forever inscribed by the angel: "He has risen! He is not here."

Those ladies were looking for Jesus among the dead—the right person but the wrong location! He is among the living. Many people still search for Jesus in the wrong places. Our Christian symbol is not a dead, lifeless body hanging on an ancient cross, but *Christ risen, trampling a broken cross beneath His feet!*

Not simply a figure in a book, Jesus is a living Person. You may study the story of Jesus as you would a biography of any other historical person. Yet, you must meet Him face-to-face. Jesus is not a memory. He is a living presence. Memories fade, but Jesus abides forever. After the Resurrection, those first Christians knew Jesus as present in their midst—present more intimately and meaningfully than even during His earthly ministry. God's mightiest deed of all time had overcome the finality of the Cross!

The real Christian is not one who knows all *about* Jesus, but one who *knows* Jesus. Jesus is not among the dead. He resides among the living! Look for Jesus in the midst of God's people.

"GO AND TELL!"

The angel of the Lord instructed, "Go, tell his disciples and Peter" (Mark 16:7). A living Christ needs witnesses. The Good News should not be a protected story locked away from people who don't appreciate its precious truth. The Good News is not a formal lecture delivered in a stained-glass voice. People who know the joy of the resurrected Jesus have received a heartfelt commission to "go and tell!" In fact, it's hard to keep it to yourself—but you can do it.

Jesus' parting words to His disciples at His ascension into heaven were, "Go into all the world and preach the good news to all creation" (Mark 16:15). Jesus planned for us to go "gossiping the gospel." We have something worth sharing. We're not hesitant to tell a friend about a good product or discovery. How much more can we happily pass the word of a risen Lord!

Our Lord "is faithful and just and will forgive us our sins and purify us from all unrighteousness" (1 John 1:9). Our Jesus says, "You will receive power when the Holy Spirit comes on you; and you will be my witnesses in Jerusalem, and in all Judea and Samaria, and to the ends of the earth" (Acts 1:8). How much our communities need to hear about Jesus!

The angel said, "Go and tell." Tell of His love, His mercy, and His comfort—but whatever you do, tell it with life! The only difference between a mudhole and a geyser is enthusiasm! Those apostles were intoxicated with an enthusiasm and zest for living until those "wanted men" became missionaries and martyrs. With deep conviction, they believed in the resurrection of Jesus.

Reichel was conducting the choir's dress rehearsal of Handel's *Messiah*. The chorus had sung through to the passage in which the soprano takes up the refrain, "I know that my Redeemer liveth."

The soloist's technique was magnificent. She had perfect breath control. Her note placement was accurate. Her enunciation of the words was flawlessly clear. After her last note, choir members glanced at the conductor's face to see his look of approval.

Instead, he stopped the orchestra, walked up to the singer, and with sorrowful eyes, he said, "Daughter, do you really believe that your Redeemer lives? Do you?"

She stammered: "Why, yes. I think so."

"Then sing it!" cried the conductor. "Tell it to me so I will know, so that all who hear you will know the joy of Christ!"

The orchestra began again. The soprano reached down deep into her heart and sang the truth as she experienced it inside. People listening then wept under the impact of her personal message: "I know that my Redeemer liveth."

The old conductor approached her with tear-dimmed eyes. "You *do* know. You have told me."

The angel says, "In your own way, now, *'Go and tell!'*"

"HE GOES BEFORE YOU!"

After the Last Supper, Jesus and His disciples walked up to the hillside Garden of Gethsemane. Jesus said to them, "After that I am risen, I will go before you into Galilee" (Mark 14:28, KJV).

Now that Jesus had arisen from the grave, the angel reminded them: "But go, tell his disciples and Peter, 'He is going ahead of you into Galilee. There you will see him, just as he told you'" (Mark 16:7).

Wherever Jesus tells us to go, whatever tasks He gives us, whenever we face difficulties in His service, He goes before us. The New Testament Greek phrase "He is going ahead of you" can be translated, "I will lead you, or put myself at the head of your company and be your Leader."

At Easter we celebrate God's trustworthiness. The good news of the Resurrection announces that Jesus is alive here and now. Jesus is no longer confined to one race or to the narrow boundaries of Israel. He is available now to the person in Hong Kong, Sidney, Vienna, Rome, or Spokane.

I had the privilege of speaking at a Methodist church for a Good Friday service. At the close of worship, two ladies and a small boy came to the pastor's study, where several of us were visiting. The younger lady called for her pastor, the Episcopal priest, to come and speak to her little boy.

The lad had seen a movie a few days earlier that dramatically portrayed the crucifixion of Jesus. With his very own eyes, he had seen Jesus crucified and buried in the tomb. His question was serious: "Since Jesus is dead, why do we have church anymore?"

In his perception, Jesus had been defeated. But that little boy had seen only part of the message: "Jesus defeated!" Thank God, the clouds have lifted and we can see the complete message: "Jesus defeated death!"

Afflicted with Down's syndrome, Philip knew he was diferent from other children. Even at Sunday School he was not fully accepted by the other nine children.

His creative teacher came up with an interesting idea. The Sunday following Easter, he brought 10 empty pantyhose containers—the ones that look like big eggs. Since it was a beautiful spring day, he took the children outside and asked each one to find a symbol of new life and put it into an egg—an empty pantyhose container.

As the children gathered back into the classroom, the eggs filled with their secrets of new life were mixed up and then one by one opened by the teacher. The 10 children were delighted as each one was opened and revealed its secret contents to illustrate new life. A flower. A butterfly. Then the teacher opened one that was completely empty—nothing in it. The children expressed disappointment, but Philip tugged on the teacher's shirt. "It's mine!"

The children reacted with childish put-down: "You don't ever do things right, Philip—there's nothing in there!"

Philip defended himself: "I did so. I did it right. It's empty—the tomb is empty!"

A long silence of insight followed—and suddenly Philip was a part of that group for sure.

That summer Philip died. His funeral was held at the church. Insight gave birth to action. Nine little children with their teacher marched up to the altar bringing not flowers, but an empty egg—an empty, discarded pantyhose container.[1]

Philip had indeed taught them the completed message: "Jesus defeated death."

Fear not. For He is not here: He is risen! Here's the greatest discovery I ever made: I serve a risen Savior!

Notes

Chapter 1

1. E. Stanley Jones, *Victory Through Surrender* (Nashville: Abingdon Press, 1966), 124.

2. H. S. Vigeveno, *Jesus the Revolutionary* (Glendale, Calif.: Regal Books, 1966), 101-2.

3. C. S. Cowles, "The Pastor Deals with Failure," *Preacher's Magazine,* January 1976, 7.

4. William Barclay, ed., *The Gospel of Luke,* in *The Daily Study Bible Series* (Philadelphia: Westminster Press, 1956), 283.

5. Ibid.

6. Charles L. Allen, *Healing Words* (Westwood, N.J.: Fleming H. Revell Company, 1961), 101.

7. Jones, *Victory Through Surrender,* 128.

Chapter 2

1. William Ernest Henry, "Invictus," in *The Best Loved Poems of the American People,* selected by Hazel Felleman (Garden City, N.Y.: Doubleday & Co., 1936).

2. Charles L. Wallis, ed., *The Table of the Lord* (New York: Harper and Brothers, 1958), 145.

3. E. Stanley Jones, *Abundant Living* (New York: Abingdon Press, 1942), 144.

4. C. Neil Strait, *Words of Men at the Cross* (Kansas City: Beacon Hill Press of Kansas City, 1970), 23.

5. William E. McCumber, *Beacon Bible Expositions* (Kansas City: Beacon Hill Press of Kansas City, 1975), 1:203.

6. Marcia Skinner, "Jesus for Us," *World Mission,* July 1976, 5.

7. Reprinted from *Say It with Love,* 14-15, by Howard G. Hendricks, published by Victor Books, 1972, SP Publications, Inc., Wheaton, Ill.

8. Harry Milton Taylor, *Faith Must Be Lived* (New York: Harper and Brothers, 1951), 52.

Chapter 3

1. Barclay, *The Gospel of Luke,* 282.

2. William Barclay, *The Gospel of Matthew,* in *The Daily Study Bible Series* (Philadelphia: Westminster Press, 1957), 2:383.

3. George Arthur Buttrick, ed., *The Interpreter's Bible* (New York: Abingdon Press, 1952), 8:763.

4. Barclay, *The Gospel of Luke,* 281.

5. Ibid.

6. George W. Truett, *The Salt of the Earth,* ed. Powhatan W. James (Grand Rapids: Wm. B. Eerdmans Publishing Co., 1949), 90.

7. Barclay, *The Gospel of Luke,* 281.

8. William Barclay, *The Gospel of John,* in *The Daily Study Bible Series* (Philadelphia: Westminster Press, 1955), 2:270.

9. G. Campbell Morgan, *Studies in the Four Gospels* (Old Tappan, N.J.: Fleming H. Revell Co., 1931), 254.

10. Strait, *Words of Men at the Cross,* 28.

11. Kenneth L. Chafin and Lloyd J. Ogilvie, ed., *The Communicator's Commentary* (Waco, Tex.: Word Books, 1985), 7:28.

Chapter 4

1. Clarence Edward Macartney, *More Sermons from Life* (Nashville: Cokesbury Press, 1939), 166.

2. Buttrick, ed., *The Interpreter's Bible,* 7:897.

3. Ibid., 895-96.

4. Ibid., 897.

5. William Edward Biederwolf, *Later Evangelistic Sermons* (Chicago: Bible Institute Colportage Assoc., 1925), 23-24.

6. Harry Emerson Fosdick, *Riverside Sermons* (New York: Harper and Brothers, 1958), 311.

7. Ibid.

8. Hyman J. Appelman, *God's Answer to Man's Sin* (Grand Rapids: Zondervan Publishing House, 1950), 60.

Chapter 5

1. Reprinted from *Collected Verse of Edgar A. Guest,* by Edgar A. Guest (Chicago: Contemporary Books, 1934), 732-33. Used by permission of Contemporary Books. All rights reserved.

2. William Barclay, *The Gospel of Mark,* in *The Daily Study Bible Series* (Philadelphia: Westminster Press, 1954), 376.

3. Roy and Revel Hession, *The Calvary Road* (Fort Washington, Pa.: Christian Literature Crusade, n.d.), 42.

4. Strait, *Words of Men at the Cross,* 35.

5. Don Richardson, *Eternity in Their Hearts* (Ventura, Calif.: Regal Books, 1981), 117.

Chapter 6

1. Reginald E. O. White, *The Stranger of Galilee* (Grand Rapids: Wm. B. Eerdmans Publishing Co., 1960), 93.

2. Appelman, *God's Answer to Man's Sin,* 61-65.

Chapter 7

1. A. W. Tozer, *Man: The Dwelling Place of God* (Harrisburg, Pa.: Christian Publications, 1966), 171.

2. McCumber, *Beacon Bible Expositions,* 1:214.

3. Barclay, *The Gospel of Luke,* 295.

4. E. Stanley Jones, *A Song of Ascents: A Spiritual Autobiography* (Nashville: Abingdon Press, 1968), 89.

5. Adapted from *Knight's Treasury of Illustrations,* comp. Walter B. Knight (Grand Rapids: Wm. B. Eerdmans Publishing Co., 1963), 100.

Chapter 8

1. Quoted in Russell Bradley Jones, *Calvary Attitudes* (Grand Rapids: Baker Book House, 1958), 39.

2. Ibid., 43.

3. John Schmidt, *The Gospel According to Strange Evangelists* (Grand Rapids: Zondervan Publishing House, 1939), 88.

4. John Guest and Lloyd J. Ogilvie, ed., *The Communicator's Commentary, Old Testament* (Waco, Tex.: Word Books, 1988), 17:123-24. © 1988, Word, Inc. Used by permission. All rights reserved.

Chapter 9

1. Andrew W. Blackwood, *Planning a Year's Pulpit Work* (New York: Abingdon Press, 1952), 120.

2. C. H. Spurgeon, *Our Lord's Passion and Death* (London: Passmore and Alabaster, 1904), 627.

3. Robert Frost, "The Road Not Taken," in *Twentieth-Century American Poetry,* ed. Conrad Aiken (New York: The Modern Library, 1944), 66.

4. Richard E. Howard, *Newness of Life* (Kansas City: Beacon Hill Press of Kansas City, 1975), 82.

5. H. D. M. Spence and Joseph S. Exell, ed., *St. Luke, The Pulpit Commentary* (New York: Funk and Wagnalls Co., 1908), 2:242.

Chapter 10

1. A. F. Harper, ed., *Beacon Bible Commentary* (Kansas City: Beacon Hill Press, 1964), 6:249.

Chapter 11

1. Raymond C. Ortlund, *Intersections: With Christ at the Crossroads of Life* (Waco, Tex.: Word Books, 1979), 111.

2. H. D. M. Spence and Joseph S. Exell, ed., *St. Mark, The Pulpit Commentary* (New York: Funk and Wagnalls, 1907), 2:310.

3. James S. Stewart, *The Life and Teaching of Jesus Christ* (New York: Abingdon Press, n.d.), 171.

4. Ibid., 172.

5. William Barclay, *The Mind of Jesus* (New York: Harper and Brothers, 1960), 262.

6. Jones, *Calvary Attitudes* , 78.

7. Ernest Borgnine, "At the Foot of the Cross," *Guideposts,* March 1989, 78.

Chapter 12

1. Barclay, *The Gospel of Mark,* 386.

2. Truett, *The Salt of the Earth,* 109-110.

3. Clarence Edward Macartney, *Macartney's Illustrations: Illustrations from*

the Sermons of Clarence Edward Macartney (New York: Abingdon-Cokesbury Press, 1945), 29.

Chapter 13

1. Adapted from *The Communicator's Commentary,* Vol. NT 8:296-98, by Maxie D. Dunnam, Lloyd J. Ogilvie, gen. ed., © 1982, Word, Inc., Dallas, Texas. Used by permission. All rights reserved.

Bibliography

Adkins, Ronald. "You Save My Life," "By All Means—Save Some." *Herald of Holiness* (unidentified issue and date), 20.

Allen, Charles L. *Healing Words.* Westwood, N.J.: Fleming H. Revell Co., 1961.

Appelman, Hyman J. *God's Answer to Man's Sin.* Grand Rapids: Zondervan Publishing House, 1950.

Barclay, William. *The Gospel of John.* In *The Daily Study Bible Series.* Philadelphia: Westminster Press, 1955.

———. *The Gospel of Luke.* In *The Daily Study Bible Series.* Philadelphia: Westminster Press, 1956.

———. *The Gospel of Mark.* In *The Daily Study Bible Series.* Philadelphia: Westminster Press, 1954.

———. *The Gospel of Matthew,* vol. 2. In *The Daily Study Bible Series.* Philadelphia: Westminster Press, 1957.

Blackwood, Andrew W. *Planning a Year's Pulpit Work.* New York: Abingdon Press, 1952.

Borgnine, Ernest. "At the Foot of the Cross." *Guideposts,* March 1989.

Buttrick, George Arthur, ed. *The Interpreter's Bible,* vol. 7. New York: Abingdon Press, 1951.

Chafin, Kenneth L., and Lloyd J. Ogilivie, ed. *The Communicator's Commentary,* vol. 7. Waco, Tex.: Word Books, 1985.

Fosdick, Harry Emerson. *Riverside Sermons.* New York: Harper and Brothers, 1958.

Guest, Edgar A. *Favorite Verse of Edgar A. Guest.* New York: Permabooks, 1950.

Guest, John, and Lloyd J. Ogilvie, ed. *The Communicator's Commentary, Old Testament,* vol. 17. Waco, Tex.: Word Books, 1988.

Harper, A. F., ed. *Beacon Bible Commentary,* vol. 6. Kansas City: Beacon Hill Press, 1964.

Hendricks, Howard G. *Say It with Love.* Wheaton, Ill.: Victor Books, 1972.

Hession, Roy and Revel. *The Calvary Road.* Fort Washington, Pa.: Christian Literature Crusade, n.d.

Howard, Richard E. *Newness of Life.* Kansas City: Beacon Hill Press of Kansas City, 1975.

Jones, E. Stanley. *Victory Through Surrender.* Nashville: Abingdon Press, 1966.

Jones, Russell Bradley. *Calvary Attitudes.* Grand Rapids: Baker Book House, 1958.

Jordan, G. Ray. *Prayer That Prevails.* New York: Macmillan Co., 1958.

McCumber, William E. *Beacon Bible Expositions,* vol. 1. Kansas City: Beacon Hill Press of Kansas City, 1975.

Ortlund, Raymond G. *Intersections: With Christ at the Crossroads of Life.* Waco, Tex.: Word Books, 1979.

Richardson, Don. *Eternity in Their Hearts.* Ventura, Calif.: Regal Books, 1981.

Sayers, Dorothy. *A Matter of Eternity.* (An unidentified source.)

Schmidt, John. *The Gospel According to Strange Evangelists.* Grand Rapids: Zondervan Publishing House, 1939.

Skinner, Marcia. "Jesus for Us." *World Mission,* July 1976, 5.

Spence, H. D. M., and Joseph S. Exell, ed. *St. Luke,* Vol. 2, *The Pulpit Commentary.* New York: Funk and Wagnalls Co., 1908.

———. *St. Mark,* Vol. 2, *The Pulpit Commentary.* New York: Funk and Wagnalls, 1907.

Spurgeon, C. H. *Our Lord's Passion and Death.* London: Passmore and Alabaster, 1904.

Stewart, James S. *The Life and Teaching of Jesus Christ.* New York: Abingdon Press, n.d.

Strait, C. Neil. *Words of Men at the Cross.* Kansas City: Beacon Hill Press of Kansas City, 1970.

Taylor, Harry Milton. *Faith Must Be Lived.* New York: Harper and Brothers, 1951.

Tozer, A. W. *Man: The Dwelling Place of God.* Harrisburg, Pa.: Christian Publications, 1966.

Vigeveno, H. S. *Jesus the Revolutionary.* Glendale, Calif.: Regal Books, 1966.

Wallis, Charles L., ed. *The Table of the Lord.* New York: Harper and Brothers, 1958.

White, Reginald E. O. *The Stranger of Galilee.* Grand Rapids: Wm. B. Eerdmans Publishing Co., 1960.